D1632161

Critical Acclaim for *Got, Not Got:*
The A-Z of Lost Football Culture, Treasures & Pleasures

The British
SportsBook12
Awards

Runner-up, Best Football Book, British Sports Book Awards 2012

"A veritable Dundee cake of a book."
Danny Kelly, talkSport

"Recalling a more innocent time before Sky Sports and millionaire players, *Got, Not Got* is like a long
soak in a warm bath of football nostalgia: an A-Z of memorabilia, ephemera and ill-advised haircuts."
In Demand, Mail on Sunday Live magazine

"The real magic is the collection and display of the illustrative material of stickers, badges, programme
covers, Subbuteo figures and other ephemera. It is astonishingly thorough, well-presented, inspired
and indeed had me going, 'yes, got, got, not got, forgot, never seen'."
When Saturday Comes

"A cracking book which whisks you back to a different footballing era."
Brian Reade, Mirror Football

"This memorabilia fest is a delightful reminder of what's gone from the game: 'magic sponges',
Subbuteo and, er, magazines for shinpads. Such innocent times, eh?"
FourFourTwo

"The book's great fun. It's an essential if you grew up watching football in the 60s, 70s or 80s.
It's a kind of football fan's catnip. Nobody can quite walk past it. They start looking at it and then
realise they've got something else they should be doing 10 or 15 minutes later."
Paul Hawksbee, talkSport.

"The best book about football written in the last 20 years."
Bill Borrows, Esquire

"A body of work that transcends being 'just a book' by a considerable distance."
In Bed With Maradona blog

"Obviously, everybody over the age of 40 is going to absolutely love this.
There's something for every fan of every club."
Andy Jacobs, talkSport

"Browsable for hours, even days, preferably with your favourite records from the 1970s in the
background, this is the Christmas present that every football fan of a certain age yearns to peruse
while their neglected partner's busy basting the turkey and getting quietly pickled on cooking sherry...
Sit back and be blissfully reminded of adverts, food products, players, toys, kits, magazines, stickers
and trends you'd long since confined to your mental attic."
Ian Plenderleith, Stay-at-Home Indie Pop blog

"I've had this for a month but haven't got round to reviewing it because it keeps disappearing.
It's the sign of a good book that people repeatedly pick it up and walk away with it.
A hardback collection of vintage football memorabilia that you need in your life...
It's like finding your old football stickers."
James Brown, SabotageTimes.com

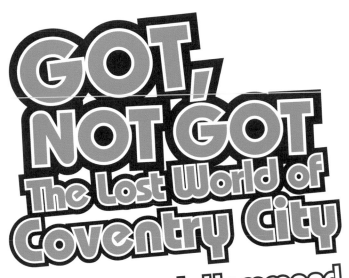

GOT, NOT GOT
The Lost World of Coventry City

Derek Hammond & Gary Silke

Pitch Publishing Ltd
A2 Yeoman Gate
Yeoman Way
Durrington
BN13 3QZ

Email: info@pitchpublishing.co.uk
Web: www.pitchpublishing.co.uk

First published by Pitch Publishing 2014
Text © 2014 Derek Hammond and Gary Silke

13-digit ISBN: 9781909626621
Design and typesetting by Olner Pro Sport Media.
Printed in the UK by CPI Group (UK), Croydon CR0 4YY

*"Several clubs in recent years have taken a leaf out of Coventry's books.
They put the requirements of their fans at the top of the list by building smart
new stands and trying to get a 'family atmosphere' at their ground – and the
money that went to buy the new stars at Coventry was provided, in the main,
by the supporters flocking into the new stands.
There must be a moral here somewhere. That old adage that fans will only
support a winning team may need revising. It may well be that ground
amenities are just as important."*

Vince Hill, 1970

*"For too long this club has shopped at Woolworth's,
from now on we'll be shopping at Harrods."*

John Sillett, 1988

ERNIE MACHIN
COVENTRY CITY

RIGHT HALF

BRIAN ALDERSON

BRIAN JOICEY
CENTRE FORWARD

Jeff Blockley
LEFT HALF

A&BC

A&BC Chewing Gum of Romford, Essex, holds a special place in the hearts of millions of big kids. Back in the 1950s, it was Douglas Coakley (the 'C' in the company name) who came up with the idea of packaging football cards with a thin slab of chewy, a combination which proved a natural winner. Throughout the 1960s and into the 1970s they produced a yearly set of football cards, as well as other stickers, tattoos and card series covering everything from the Beatles to Star Trek – and American sports and TV-related cards bound for the US via partner company, Topps.

Nowadays they're worth anything up to two or three quid each for the 1960s and early Seventies cards in excellent condition – though sadly that price drops off steeply for ones with edges chewed and worn, like ours. The 'crinkle-cut' extra photographs given away free with each pack in 1969 are even more desirable, and the little Action Transfers given away as extras in every pack in 1971 are worth anything up to seven or eight quid apiece. This for a small piece of paper which was given away in a packet that cost thruppence.

Unfortunately, in 1974, A&BC lost a long-simmering legal battle and was taken over

by Topps-Bazooka. The end of one story, and the beginning of another.

But, for some reason, it isn't easy to put out of your mind stray memories of football's long-lost people and places, the youthful obsessions and outdated rituals that seemed so important back in the day – and, in a strange way, still do. It might be a name on an email that you immediately associate with a recoloured kit on a card, and think: "Not got." Or just a vacant moment when you're whisking down the M6 at 80mph and find yourself wondering… whatever happened to Quintin Young?

It isn't everyone who could possibly understand.

COVENTRY CITY

Neil Martin
CENTRE FORWARD

Scotch missed
A decent strike rate of 40 goals in 106 for the ex-Alloa, Queen of the South and Hibs forward.

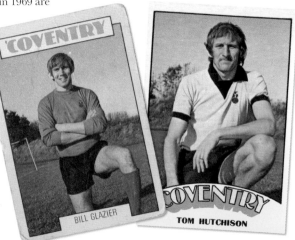

'COVENTRY

BILL GLAZIER

COVENTRY

TOM HUTCHISON

ACTION MAN

They don't make boys' toys like Action
Man any more.

Kids aren't interested in peering
through the back of a plastic doll's
head and into his 'Eagle Eye' when the
maximum thrill available is a slightly
blurred view of the back garden. And as
for realistic hair and gripping hands...
they tend to pall into insignificance
next to the Xbox's 3-D virtual world,
where it's perfectly possible to drop in

Living in a Box:
Millions of happy
hours were once spent
yearning for hot Action
Man accessories.

on Berlin in 1945 or Pluto in the year
4567, shredding Nazis and aliens alike
with a sonic fire ray akin to a red-mist
glare from Terry Yorath.

They'd call Action Man un-PC now –
an eight-inch multi-skilled terrorist who
thought nothing of changing out of his
Nazi Stormtrooper uniform into that of
a Navy frogman, a Canadian Mountie or
an astronaut. And so into his Sky Blues
kit for a kickaround with your sister's
Barbie in goal.

Unfortunately, that's when our
vicious little accomplice became a
complete bore. Whether you had one
Action Man or 22, there just wasn't a
game you could base around his non-
existent ball skills. The specific types
of 'action' mastered by 'the movable

fighting man' were limited to bending
at the joints and being blown into the
air. There was only so much fun you
could have dressing a doll in football
kit, especially as it exposed his shattered-
looking kneecaps. The final straw was the
orthopaedic stand which he needed to
balance on one leg, hovering over the ball
in a sorry personification of inaction.

Because most Action Man enthusiasts
kept their figures strictly military, the
scarcity value of the football range has
more recently seen eBay prices soaring.
Original 1960s kits are regularly sold on
the auction site for over £250, and the
little Action Man team badges given away
with the original kit pack can sell for just
as much on their own. If only Palitoy had
chosen City as one of the 'big clubs' with
their own team kit, Action Man's two-inch-
long dark blue socks could now pay for a
decent night out.

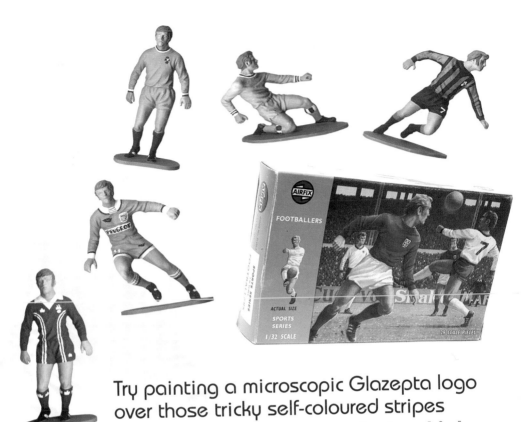

Try painting a microscopic Glazepta logo over those tricky self-coloured stripes on a bloke who's two inches high.

AIRFIX

Ever since 1955, when they released their 1/72 Spitfire model kit, Airfix had been satisfying little boys' unquenchable thirst for recreating World War II.

You could paint up a boxful of Commandos or Desert Rats and painstakingly put together a Hampden bomber, though how you were supposed to stop the 'cement' from clouding up the glass canopy of the cockpit was anyone's guess.

Even more satisfying than endless war was the 1/32nd scale Airfix Sports Series of Airfix Footballers – your chance to ditch khaki and grey for the far more exciting football colours of Cambridge blue, white and claret, and maybe even a few of those other oppo colours like yellow and puce and red.

Up until the mid-Seventies it wasn't too much trouble recreating miniature versions of the kits of the day; but things got a lot trickier after that time.

Go on, you try painting an even row of Umbro sleeve stripes or a microscopic Glazepta logo over those tricky contrasting blue stripes on a bloke who's just over two inches high.

Long boring Sunday afternoons were the perfect time for creating a pair of Umbro sock turnovers, until the double misery of *Last of the Summer Wine* and the parental enquiry: "Have you got any homework, son?" reminded you that Monday morning was nearly upon us once again.

Thanks to eBay you can still get that distinctive box through the post with England vs. Germany on the front. Old habits, like old enemies, die hard. And if you've got a steady hand and a couple of hundred hours on your hands, there's no more satisfying way to waste your time.

THE BOBBLE HAT

If you want to get ahead, get a hat. That's what optimistic types (with hats) used to say back in the olden days before the unnatural incursion of the baseball cap gave headgear in general a bad name in Britain. Like greedy, stupid grey squirrels ganging up and bullying our delightful native red squirrels, the ubiquitous baseball cap soon put paid to the bowler, the trilby, the boater and the humble club-coloured bobble hat, which was once the universal signifier of a football fan.

Nowadays you see more Peruvian tea cosies and furry Russian hats than good old British bobbles at the Ricoh. Yet even such fancy-dress items exhibit more style than the baseball cap, which instantly infantilises its wearer, marks him out as a man without imagination or wit, and automatically devalues every sentence he utters.

Bring back the bobble! – as modelled here by decent men of Warwickshire sporting ties, blouson jackets and/or sheepskin, as the footballing gods intended.

And yet we'd probably fight shy of attempting to reintroduce the full-face football balaclava helmet, eh?

SUN SOCCERCARDS

Allow us to whisk you back to the tail end of the 70s, and one particular night beloved of many football card collectors. The night in question was notable for the long, gruelling, coffee-fuelled marathon undertaken by the anonymous Sun Soccercard artist, chained to his desk with a dozen packs of big bright felt pens and ordered to produce a set of nearly 1,000 player likenesses (or as near as possible).

M. COOP (Coventry City)

B. McDONALD (Coventry City)

The legendary felt-pen artist
never did get the hang of eyes – or heads.

The results speak for themselves. But just in case you don't recognise your heroes of yesteryear, here's... well, let's just hope their old mums don't recognise them either!

Anything to avoid paying image rights, eh? Even if the man with the felt-pen never did quite get the hang of eyes, their size relative to the human head, and the fact that they're usually pretty much on the same level.

B. POWELL (Coventry City)

M. FERGUSON (Coventry City)

L. CARTWRIGHT (Wales)

S. HUNT (Coventry City)

I. WALLACE (Scotland)

Soccercard Attack Alert! 1979 saw Sky Blues strikers Ian Wallace and Mick Ferguson entombed in huge frizzy hairballs.

THE DONKEY KICK

It could never happen now, Cov's celebrated *Match of the Day* Goal of the Season from 1970/71…

"An out-of-puff Everton defender upends Cattlin with a groin-high tackle…

"A swift talking-to, and now Coventry have a free-kick 25 yards out. It's ginger-haired Willie Carr standing astride the ball, while moustachioed Ernie Hunt, looking like a Mexican bandit, shapes to pang one goalward.

"But, my gracious! Carr has flicked the ball up backwards between his

heels… Hunt has let fly with a looping rasper… and YES! Right into the corner of the net over goalkeeper West!

"What a sensational trick, every schoolboy in the Midlands will be trying out the 'Donkey Drop' tomorrow lunchtime…

"But hold on. The referee is receiving a message from the fourth official on his headset. He's disallowed the goal, brought back play, and has booked Carr for touching the ball twice."

"But, my gracious!
Carr has flicked the ball up backwards between his heels…
Hunt has let fly with a looping rasper… and YES!"

Ernie Hunt – and those dark-blue socks you thought we'd got wrong when we mentioned them on the Action Man page!

THE CIGARETTE CARD

In the age of No Smoking – when anyone who fancies a tab is forced to stand outside their office in all weathers, and even crowd into a ramshackle lean-to hurriedly added twixt bar and beer garden – it won't be long until kids don't even recognise the reference to a good old-fashioned gasper, already obscured by the slick, sad euphemism of 'candy stick'.

The sweetie cigarette will soon be no more, like Highfield Road, mud and the sky-high promise of Rangers' 1972 UEFA Cup Winners' Cup winner Colin Stein signing for City.

Back in the day, however, they were clearly the best option for L-plate smokers, both in terms of their unique,

Sweetie cigarette cards are already an obscurity to kids aged under 20 or 30. And the original pre-war mass cult of the cigarette card proper will soon be nothing but a memory clung to by a disappearing breed of oldsters.

No, not the stout men who smoked for England during the war only to be stamped out underfoot in the fallout from NHS cost-cutting exercises determined to make everyone live to 200. But us, the jammy-faced kids who remember the well-thumbed contents of Granddad's hand-me-down baccy tin.

We posed manfully with a sugary cig dangling from our lips, fooling absolutely everybody.

chalky-sweet flavour and cunning authenticity, courtesy of a dab of pink food colouring on the burning 'hot' end. And they came with a football card, too, if you were lucky – or a fat cricketer or lady tennis player if the dreaded mixed-sports set was in season.

Barratt's and Bassett's packs of sweet cigarettes were a throwback to the cigarette cards that had died out in the war; but we never realised that at the time. We were too busy posing manfully with our sugary cig dangling from our lips, fooling absolutely everybody.

Guess Which Club:
The clue, as Jim Bowen
might have said, is in
the question.

13

JIMMY HILL'S SKY BLUE REVOLUTION

Taking over late in 1961, the great moderniser Jimmy Hill began a PR onslaught, introducing Britain's first continental-style one-colour kit, changing the club nickname from boring Bantams to mod-sounding Sky Blues, and leading the Third Division also-rans on a six-season romp up the leagues.

"Between us, we took excitement into the Third Division towns throughout England," he wrote in his 1966 New Year programme notes. "We turned League matches into Cup ties, drab monotony into fervent patriotism. The strains of 'The Sky Blue Song' and the chants of 'Coventry City Cha-Cha-Cha'

Hill Side: So much to look forward to
— including those revolutionary 2.45
Saturday kick-offs!

COVENTRY CITY

OFFICIAL PROGRAMME

SIX PENCE

often woke up local fans to reply just as noisily..."

Hill introduced the Sky Blue Express supporters' train, and organised the first big-screen beambacks to Highfield Road as early as 1965. He rode a white horse around the Highfield Road pitch – mercifully his only Lady Godiva reference – personally overseeing the doling out of free Bovril and tea at half-time from Sky Blue backpacks.

"We had started a revolution which was to reverberate around football. Some clubs wagged jealous tongues and ridiculed our so-called gimmicks; some journalists, too, who had willingly used our kinky stories in the headlines..."

He arranged 'pop and crisp' days for local kids to meet the stars, and took the lead in corporate entertainment, signing up 'leading local business people' as Vice President's Club members. Before the match and at half-time, Sky Blue Radio rocked the tinny PA system: yet another famous first that was destined to catch on.

Job done, Hill quit for a career in the hot new arena of TV football two days before the Sky Blues' debut in the top flight.

Killer was no yob,
He was a loyal and faithful servant.

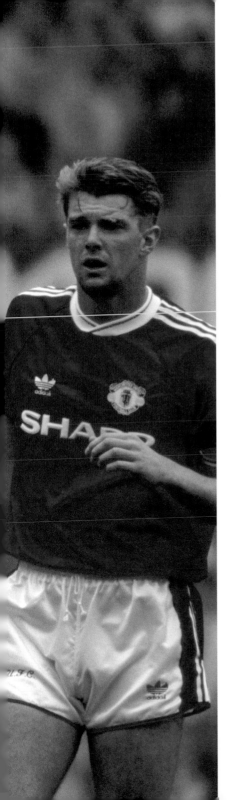

THE TENACIOUS WARRIOR

The nominated hard man of each club used to be almost as celebrated as the star strikers they sought to bruise. We're talking players you loved to hate – unless they happened to be on your side, in which case there was often room for a small amount of give-and-take. A healthy alternative perspective on their tendency towards ultraviolence.

Take Brian 'Killer' Kilcline, for example: he was a warrior, a loyal servant for seven years, and a man you'd want to go to war with, but certainly not against. He may have had a leg hanging on by gristle, but the skipper still limped up the Wembley steps to claim the FA Cup.

Oppo fans were often incensed by Killer's high spirits, by his tenacious, uncompromising tackling and never-say-die attitude – not to mention his luxuriant bubble perm and later fulsome mullet in combo with a big bristly tash (even today he bears a remarkable resemblance to Lemmy).

There seemed to be a complicit understanding between a good old-fashioned hard man and referee whereby no one could be booked in the opening five minutes of a game. He was allowed one free, 'welcoming' clog on an opposing forward's calf, 'just to let them know I'm here'.

The second, Achilles-crunching challenge might warrant a brief word of warning from the ref. The third might occasionally earn a booking, at which the defender would present a picture of outraged innocence.

By this stage, the talented striker had completely lost:
1 – stomach for the contest; or,
2 – all feeling below the waist.
And the job was a good 'un.

DENIM JACKET PATCHES

Back in the day, no self-respecting teenager would be seen at a football match or out on the town without a denim jacket rendered almost invisible under the weight of Coffer sew-on patches down the back and arms.

The very sight of these vintage 1970s patches is almost enough to make

How do kids today advertise their love of Northern Soul, Motorhead

or Ian Wallace's ginger afro?

anybody start nagging their mum to stitch as many embroidered cartoon elephants as humanly possible on to their parka sleeves and Army Surplus schoolbag.

When we first mentioned our weakness for Coffer paraphernalia to Sky Blues supercollector Dean Gordon, he sent us a great pile of patches and badges by return of mail. We were inundated with enough enamel and frayed vintage cotton to weigh down the denim jackets of half the Kop on a

blustery afternoon circa 1978. What do kids today do now they can't advertise their love of Northern Soul, Motorhead or Ian Wallace's ginger afro via their denim jacket? Ah yes, there's always that new-fangled internet.

I'M A CITY NUT, indeed. COVENTRY CITY TURN ME ON.

UP! COVENTRY

Levis

No. 1 COVENTRY CITY F.C.

COVENTRY CITY F.C. SKY BLUES

Cotton is perfectly soft and natural,
alternately warm and cool,
and shrink resistant.

COTTON

It's the sensual associations that come bundled with cotton that make it such a rich source of minor, if largely subconscious, pleasure.

Ahh, the smell of a new cotton T-shirt being pulled on over your head on a Friday night. The slow fade of a favourite shirt, laundered a hundred times by your mum. Cotton next to the skin – warm against the winter cold, cool in summer... the pure smell of plain sky blue, a simple embroidered City elephant-on-a-football crest, and no other labels or logos smelling of a modern attempt to cash in.

In 150 years, the only negatives against cotton were an association with hippie cheesecloth and, ah yes, the institutionalised horrors of the slave trade.

Cotton isn't just perfect for clothes because it's easy to take care of and to wash. It's soft because it's made out of perfectly natural fluff. And it's cheap because the fluff grows on trees.

And so some tiresome bean counter inevitably decided to put about the idea that cotton is altogether second rate. Wear it for sports and it apparently now soaks up sweat in a way that you wouldn't want it to be soaked up. Cotton isn't stretchy enough, and it needs ironing, unlike a certain artificial wonder-fabric. They even tried to convince us that shell-suit bottoms were cooler and more comfortable than jeans.

Now, it just so happens that while cotton is cheap, polyester is cheaper. So much cheaper, it's practically free.

Polyester is an artificial plastic made from the acids and alcohol produced when you torch petroleum – in other words, from exhaust fumes.

Polyester is hard-wearing primarily because it's hard. It's rough to the touch, keeps you cold in winter and hot in summer. Wear it in summer, or for sports, and it will make you smell like you've been dead for a week.

Bring back cotton football shirts!

CLUBCALL

Back in the Eighties and Nineties, it was the sheer unavailability of up-to-the-minute club information that made it so tantalising. So valuable.

You wouldn't want everyone else to know that Graham Oakey had a hammy, would you? – not if you were still thinking he might be playing Saturday. You wouldn't want to miss what 'Wantaway' Mick Ferguson had allegedly denied this morning – or boss Gordon Milne's counter-denials of any new ace striker rumours. Ahh, the rumours...

The Clubcall service came as a blessing for all fans – especially those exiled from local news and those trapped at work with the benefit of a free phone to avoid the disgraceful premium call rates.

At the end of the line – literally – was a local newspaper stringer (or at least an Ansafone recording of him) summing up back-page stories from yesterday's evening paper and this morning's tabs. To deliver value for money, he also used to make up juicy filler on the spot, and read it out. S-l-o-w-l-y.

"Hello... and it's a big... Sky Blues... welcome... to your exclusive... front-line... Clubcall service for... Coventry City... Football... Club.

"Listen to... Clubcall... for all the latest... news... and... information..."

Because we were paying by the second.

108 **TOMMY HUTCHISON**

112 **BARRY POWELL**

THE WONDERFUL WORLD OF SOCCER STARS

How many sets of football cards and stickers do you reckon might have been pushed out into the UK market to mark the occasion of the 1966 World Cup? Ten? Twenty? The answer, you might be surprised to hear, is none. Not a one. Zero.

In recent years a limited test production of A&BC World Cup stamps has emerged, but these are priceless rarities that had no real impact. Even though pocket-size cardboard football cards had been successfully covering the domestic game since the end of the 50s, and European and South American manufacturers had produced trailblazing sticker books for the 1962 finals, it simply didn't occur to anyone to build on these trends.

It was only when England secured Monsieur Rimet's small gold trophy that the enthusiasm really rocketed, kick-starting the British football industry in the stands, in the shops and in sticker albums up and down the country.

In the second half of the 60s, playgrounds rocked to the tribal rhythm of "Got, got, got, got, *not got*" as kids flicked through their teetering piles in search of that elusive John Tudor, perfectly willing to exchange 200 swaps to fill in the one remaining square left on their checklist.

If us Brits were slow off the mark seeing the possibilities in the market for cards and World Cups, it took even longer to get the ball rolling on the Euro-led non-sticky sticker front.

In 1967, FKS's *Wonderful World of Soccer Stars* rolled into limited, regional production, reflecting a Golden Age when all you needed to start up business in the football sticker

Founded: 1883. Ground: Highfield Road. Manager: Gordon Milne.

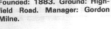

COVENTRY CITY

JIM BLYTH

LES CARTWRIGHT

CHRIS CATTLIN

MICK COOP

JOHN CRAVEN

DA

PICTURE ST

BOBBY GRAHAM — ERNIE HUNT — MIKE McGUIRE — DENNIS MORTIMER

BOB PARKER — BILL RAFFERTY — WILF SMITH — QUINTIN YOUNG

Founded: 1883. Ground: Highfield Road. Manager: Gordon Milne.

market was a picture deal with an agency – no worries if the images were a season or two out of date, that's what retouching brushes are for – and a distribution deal around the corner shops of Britain.

The idea took off, and 1968 saw the first widely available sticker set, largely repeating the previous year's mugshot efforts. The following season's largely accidental mix of action shots and head-and-shoulders upped the excitement greatly and has rarely been bettered, still offering a real window into the Wonderful, and sadly Lost World of Football in the Sixties.

The business model was clear. Give any football-mad child a packet of (not really very accurately titled) stickers, an album and a pot of Gloy gum, let him stick his first sticker into the allotted slot, surrounded by another dozen blank spaces taunting him, and let nature take its course....

CHRIS CATTLIN

JOHN CRAVEN

BILL GLAZIER — ALAN GREEN

SOCCER STARS '76 '77

20p

BUM

Founded: 1883
Ground: Highfield Road
Manager: Noel Cantwell
League Champions: Nil; F.A. Cup: Nil

COVENTRY CITY

JEFF BLOCKLEY

WILLIE CARR

DAVE CLEMENTS

MIKE COOP

BILL GLAZIER

Straight from the Elephant's Trunk!

More revelations from WestEnder's own City analyst

FANZINES

Following on from the Seventies' music-led revolutions in DIY publishing, it took a while for football to catch up, but eventually fans took to their cranky old typewriters, hunting and pecking and ker-chinging out their frustrations, and learning all-new reprographic skills along the way.

They were tired of hearing 'The Fans' View' expressed second hand in the media, where the final word, the final edit, was always predictably happy and safe. Before the 1980s, every word written about football came from an industry perspective – tapped out by writers who were paid by newspapers, magazines, television companies or club programmes, which were in turn reliant on the FA, the League or the clubs themselves.

It's a tough job, running the back page of a local paper without access to news information, player interviews or pictures.

No such problem for the first wave of fanzine rebels, who offered an all-new diet of uncensored opinion cut with terrace humour, finally putting the majority view of 20,000 regulars above the handful of professionals and hired hands – the chairman, the players, the manager, the gentlemen of the press box – who were just passing through.

Suddenly your familiar old programme seller had a bit of competition on the streets from titles such as *Sky Blue Army*, *Gary Mabbutt's Knee* and *The WestEnder*.

No matter if they were presented under headlines written using felt-pen, Letraset or John Bull Printing Outfit No. 7: here, for the very first time in print, were negative as well as positive views on our beloved clubs and teams, jokes at our own expense, better jokes at the expense of Blues and Leicester, album and gig reviews, stories of away trips, pubs and pies... always pies.

And, somewhere along the way, we discovered it wasn't just the fans in our corner of our ground who felt the same way about all-seater stadiums and ID cards, about the wreckers who came to football to chuck bananas and seats on the pitch, and the wreckers who came bearing calculators. And pies.

The WestEnder

No 10   **Coventry's independent soccer magazine**   **50p**

STRUGGLING RESERVE TEAM STRIKER *STEVE LIVINGSTONE* FEARS HE WILL NEVER MAKE THE BREAKTHROUGH INTO THE *FIRST TEAM!*
  BUT ONE DAY WHILE RETRIEVING A BALL FROM UNDERNEATH THE FLOODLIGHTS...

ZAPP!

...YOUNG LIVINGSTONE IS HIT BY A LIVE ELECTRIC CABLE, CAUSING *MILLIONS OF VOLTS* TO *SURGE* THROUGH HIS BODY. AT ONCE, HE IS TRANSFORMED INTO *ACE STRIKER* —

LIVO-MAN!

All Mod Cons
One day, all stadiums would be made like this...

SACRED TURF

Highfield Road was totally transformed in the 60s during the Jimmy Hill era, in a manner befitting the country's first truly modern football club.

Here's the Sky Blue Stand on Thackall Street going up section by section. It was started in 1963 and finished in 1964, and to say it featured all mod cons would be an understatement of a kind rarely found in an estate agent's or architect's plans.

It boasted a trendy vaulted roof and moulded plastic seats with expensive wooden trimmings of a kind only known at the time to those who had frequented a Scandinavian sauna.

The Sky Blue Stand bypassed boring old modernism and dived straight into futurism. One day, all stadiums would be made like this...

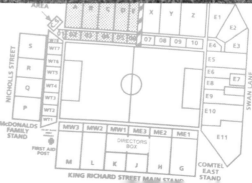

Just one slight problem: it didn't quite turn out to be the future, as the roof was discovered to have defects and it was replaced with a flat one in 1970.

Still, even today, the sight of a player trotting out of the tunnel with an all-wooden backdrop on an FKS sticker can literally be enough to make you pine for the past.

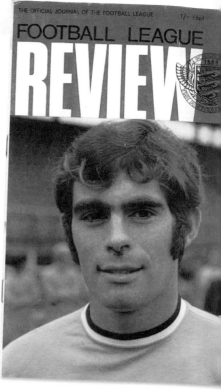

THE OFFICIAL JOURNAL OF THE FOOTBALL LEAGUE 1/- (5p)

FOOTBALL LEAGUE
REVIEW

THE FOOTBALL LEAGUE REVIEW

Run from the back bedroom of secretary Alan Hardaker's Blackpool bungalow, the Football League was devoted to showing everyone what a big, happy family their 92-member club was. The *Football League Review* was a feelgood customer mag, given away free inside club programmes, where it bolstered many four- or eight-page lower-league efforts. The *FLR* was conspicuous in its absence from several larger League grounds, where power brokers were already wary of growing League influence.

However, in stark comparison to the petty politicking backstabbing golf-clubbing small-minded scrap-metal

All change: Sky Black 'n' Greens eclipse the lilywhites of Tottenham.

League FOOTBALL

5p

merchant football-club owners of the 1970s, fans dug the freebies to bits – especially if John O'Rourke featured on the cover.

The *Review* was 5 pence 'when bought separately'; which is to say never. It was full of behind-the-scenes peeks at the day-to-day running of all the League clubs, an article on the bootroom at Barrow being just as likely as a visit to the Arsenal trophy room. Then and now, its allure was almost entirely down to staff photographer Peter Robinson, who spent whole seasons travelling around snapping mascots at Mansfield and tea-ladies in Tranmere, thinking up ever more unusual formations for his teamgroups.

"I was conscious that I was different when I talked with other photographers at games," he told *When Saturday Comes.* Robinson never missed an angle, an expression, an oddity or a location, showing more interest in football culture than the game itself.

Photoshop Schmotoshop. From Leeds' Irish midfielder to Sky Blues' long-serving German full-back in the blink of an eye.

The Review was 5 pence 'when bought separately'; which is to say never.

"I felt that you didn't just have to start photographing when the ref blew his whistle. I was interested in the whole build-up to the game."

HASTILY RECOLOURED KIT

Although there was a lot less movement in the transfer market than today, the photo agencies that supplied the football card and sticker manufacturers in the Sixties and Seventies were rarely bang up-to-date.

Cue the burning of midnight oil as heads were snipped off and reapplied to new team-mates' bodies, and old shirts hastily penned

DAVID CROSS

with new colours. Or, in the peculiar case of Tommy Booth, a perfect new set of bosoms.

You've got to love bodge jobs like this Sixties FKS sticker of Johnny Giles at the Leeds training ground, which was then subject to an inhumane Dr. Frankenstein session to become… Dietmar Bruck of the Sky Blues!

FKS albums even carried a straight-faced 'guarantee': 'In order to maintain authenticity, some of the players have been photographed in clothing which is not necessarily their official club colours'.

ITV SUNDAY AFTERNOON FOOTBALL

Today an old friend emailed me an mp3 file entitled 'Star'.

I instantly recognised the blaring, barely-in-control brass section of the *Star Soccer* theme tune and was transported back to a mid-Seventies Sunday afternoon at two o'clock.

The Sunday dinner that had taken Mum hours to cook was wolfed down in two minutes. Roast beef and Yorkshire puddings lay in my stomach, barely chewed, as I rushed to turn on the old black-and-white telly so that it would warm up in time for that blasting fanfare, played over a backdrop of one

Remember the theme tune from ATV's *Star Soccer?*

of the many Midlands First Division grounds, and the welcoming South Midland baritone of commentator Hugh Johns – a dark-chestnut, favourite-uncle tone underscored with a hint of Naval-issue cigarettes.

There was little room for manoeuvre in the editing suite, back then. The main game, however incident-packed or dull, ran for fifteen minutes up to a half-time ad break, followed by another quarter of an hour for the second half.

Part three brought fifteen minutes of a game from another ITV region. Granada's Gerald Sinstadt was the voice of *Kick Off*; Tyne Tees was Kenneth Wolstenholme on *Shoot*, while LWT's *The Big Match* was fronted by Brian Moore...

After part four's brief highlights of another game – usually Norwich or Ipswich from Anglia's *Match of the Week* with Gerry Harrison – and a round-up of results, the weekend seemed almost over.

Dozens of games went untelevised every weekend between 1969 and 1983 and that's why seeing your team was so special. With perhaps only two or three TV appearances in a lean year, the novelty never wore off.

Afternoon Delight: Roast beef, Yorkshire pud and good old Hugh Johns.

CARS IN THE GROUND

Here's a great pic recalling Highfield Road favourite Tommy Hutchison and the atmosphere inside the old ground. But peer into the background, and the image also recalls the line of invalid carriages that always used to line up in the corner of the pitch, their owners actually allowed to drive their little sky-blue three-wheelers around the cinder track and into position before kick-off.

Whatever happened to invalid carriages? Remember, they used to be steered not with a wheel but with a joystick lever action?

How come they only ever seemed to be spotted pitchside at Highfield Road and Maine Road, Manchester? Was it just clubs that played in sky blue who welcomed a select few of their disabled supporters to get involved in this front-row, thick-of-the-action manner?

Or were the 'trikes' built locally by Reliant – responsible for the famous Robin three-wheelers beloved of Del-Boy Trotter – and so that's how their got their spot by the corner flag?

So many nostalgic questions, so little useful information…

Which way did he go? Tommy Hutch confuses two Foxes with his dazzling fancy footwork.

LEAGUE LADDERS

Wahey! City top of the League!

But there was more to your youthful flights of League Ladder-related fantasy than mere self-centred feelgood relish. There was also the bottom of Scottish League Division Two to consider (or maybe, if you were feeling generous, the bottom of the fourth division, and the basement trapdoor beckoning into non-League Hell). That's where a good old English emotion known as *schadenfreude* took over – and where you found the other Midland First Division clubs – Blues, Villa, Forest, WBA, Stoke, Wolves, Leicester – along with Dirty Leeds and every other side that had put one over on City in the past three seasons.

Gifted to us in the build up to the season's big kick-off by *Shoot!* or *Roy of the Rovers* or one of the old-school shoot-'em-up comics such as *Lion* or

Valiant, the empty league ladders came first, closely followed over a number of weeks with the small cardboard team tabs designed to be slotted into their ever-changing slot in the scheme of things.

In the days before computers, even before Teletext, the appeal of being able to stare at the league table was considerable. But, after the third or fourth week, updating your league ladders became a bit too much like hard work.

And that's when you could see what it would look like if East Fife were somehow suddenly transported to second in the League behind its natural eternal leaders. Ha! Swansea in the First Division, and Burnley in the Fourth! And all those lesser Midlands clubs mysteriously close to going out of business – pointless, crowdless and hopeless, as God intended.

Ground:
Highfield Road,
Coventry

Team tab:
Cut out and keep,
and collect the
whole set of 92!

f the new

WHO

OOT!

1st DIVISION

English League

SOCCER WEEKLY

Know all there is to know with SHOOT. Every week SHOOT will be packed with informative articles and features about every aspect of the game — photographs — colour pin-ups ...

...Nobby Stiles, some of England's...ons in Training — in full colour,...the Story...e European Cup,...bby Moo...es the first of...

...the know

SHOOT/GO

	1st DIVISION
1	COVENTRY
2	ARSENAL
3	LIVERPOOL
4	TOTTENHAM
5	IPSWICH
6	SUNDERLAND
7	WEST HAM
8	MANCHESTER U.
9	MANCHESTER C.
10	STOKE
11	EVERTON
12	NEWCASTLE
13	LEEDS
14	NORWICH
15	BIRMINGHAM
16	QUEEN'S P.R.
17	MIDDLESBRO'
18	WOLVES
19	DERBY
20	WEST BROM
21	LEICESTER
22	ASTON VILLA

2nd DIVI

1	
2	
3	
4	
5	
6	
7	
8	
9	
10	
11	
12	
13	
14	
15	
16	
17	
18	
19	
20	
21	
22	

ERS

LEAGUE

	2nd DIV
1	ST. JOHNSTONE
2	E. STIRLING
3	MORTON
4	HAMILTON A.
5	STRANRAER
6	ARBROATH
7	ALBION R.
8	COWDENBEATH
9	ALLOA
10	STIRLING A.
11	EAST FIFE
12	DUMBARTON
13	AYR U.
14	QUEEN'S PARK
	MONTROSE

PROGRESS CHART...

Position	1976						197
	AUG	SEP	OCT	NOV	DEC	JAN	FEB	M
	14 21 28	4 11 18 25	2 9 16 23 30	6 13 20 27	4 11 18 25	1 8 15 22 29	5 12 19 26	5

33

Cascades of bog roll streamed down from the stands and terracing
like tissue-paper comets.

TOILET ROLL

No sooner had the ball sent shockwaves rippling through the net than cascades of bog roll would come streaming down from the stands and terracing like tissue-paper comets. Toilet roll lodged in the net, dangled over the bar and blew around the penalty box.

It wasn't just the wilful mass littering that was an issue, but the waste of resources. Most importantly, all that bottom-related refuse represented a serious Health & Safety hazard. Did you know it's now illegal for pre-school

groups to collect up toilet-roll middles
for the little kids to make rubbish
models with? It's yet more proof of the
potential hazards lurking in toilet tissue.

Even so, we still miss the loo-roll
deluge, which always seemed a cathartic
addition to a goal celebration. Not for
us Brits the labour-intensive, flashy
South American confetti-storm. A well-
aimed Andrex was far more satisfying,
plopping down in the mud next to the
beaten goalie.

MIRRORCARDS

Back in the sunny 1971/72 season, the *Daily Mirror* was kind enough to give away a set of football cards featuring teamgroups of all 92 League clubs, plus the four Home International squads. The cards could be collected up and stuck on a large wallchart entitled 'Bobby Moore's Gallery of Soccer Sides'.

As if that weren't enough, it was then possible to order from the newspaper's HQ a special giant-size 'My Club' card to take pride of place in the middle of the poster.

Not many punters made it this far down the line — the City 'My Club' card is one of the rarest around.

To be frank, few punters made it this far down the line – making the Coventry City 'My Club' card (not to mention that of some of the smaller third and fourth division teams) one of the rarest around. Especially in mint condition, as those that were ordered were almost inevitably slapped straight on to Junior's wall!

Coventry City

Back row (*l. to r.*) : Strong, Coop, Hill, Mortimer and Hunt. Centre row (*l. to r.*) : Asprey, Joicey, Rafferty, Glazier, McManus, Cattlin, Parker and Mr. Cantwell (Manager). Seated row (*l. to r.*) : Machin, Carr, Young, Clements, Blockley, O'Rourke, Smith, Alderson and Barry.

The *Father Ted* perspective challenge: the small card is big and the big card is for away.

RY

DES

e

Back row (*l. to r.*) : Strong, Coop, Hill, Mortimer and Hunt. Centre row (*l. to r.*) : Asprey, Joicey, Rafferty, Glazier, McManus, Cattlin, Parker and Mr. Cantwell (Manager). Seated row (*l. to r.*) : Machin, Carr, Young, Clements, Blockley, O'Rourke, Smith, Alderson and Barry.

THE BANTAM BABES

Sky Blues Youth Team In Topless Teat
'Specialist' Photos Shock.

Things professional footballers would refuse to do today. Number 1 of 32: the fancy-dress photo-op.

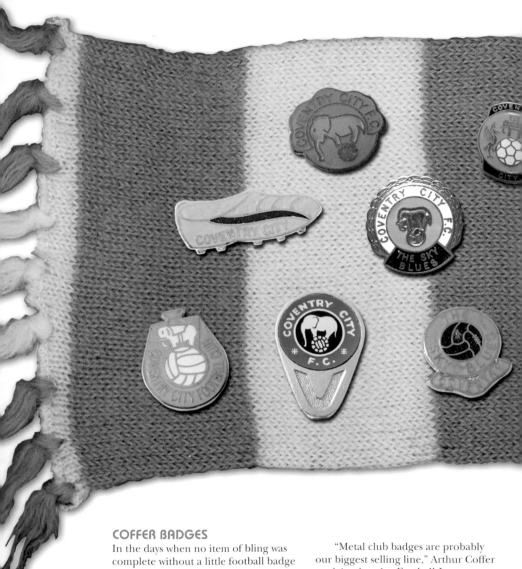

COFFER BADGES

In the days when no item of bling was complete without a little football badge or a cocky slogan, Northampton- and London-based Coffer Sports were the jewellers to a nation of kids. They had a wonderful range of pendants, identity bracelets, rings, sew-on patches, lapel badges and key-rings, all tastefully(ish) crowned with enamel club badges.

"Metal club badges are probably our biggest selling line," Arthur Coffer explained to the *Football League Review* in 1973. "For many fans the collecting of these lapel badges has developed into almost a cult. But rosettes are not far behind. We make more than half a million of them a year, in all sizes and all colours, and I

Next to Ali, CITY ARE THE GREATEST!

Coventry City, GOTTA LOTTA BOTTLE.

cannot see them losing their appeal even though there are signs that the soccer souvenir market is slowly changing."

Slowly changing? Surely not. You mean to say it's no longer the case that COVENTRY CITY GOTTA LOTTA BOTTLE? NEXT TO ALI, CITY ARE THE GREATEST!

Undercover Elephant: full of religious symbolism, and strong enough to carry Cov Castle on its back... according to coventry.gov.uk!

Book 8

THE SCRAPPER

In the six-million-year interval between man first walking upright and the invention of the 24-hour kids' TV channel, the PlayStation, the Xbox, the Wii and the DS, kids were faced with a bit of a challenge. How to fill all those long, boring hours before it was time to blow their candles out? It was merely hundreds of years ago when the penny finally dropped, and pastimes such as needlepoint, pressing wild flowers and making your own scrapbook at last began to gain popularity.

Most young football fans had a go at assembling scraps devoted to their football team, but few persisted for very long. The first page of every scrapbook is filled, the last page hardly ever. After a few weeks, cutting your club's match reports and photos out of the paper tended to become a chore, enabling you to later track the ever-decreasing degree of care with which they were Gloyed onto the coarse pages. And then there was that final time you jumped the gun and Dad found a comedy hole in the back of his *Sunday Express* before he'd finished with it.

And that's where most kids' interest in scrapbooks tends to end.

We're pleased to say that Dean Gordon didn't only persist with his City scrapbooks, but clung on to them during decades' worth of well-meaning spring-cleaning sessions.

OUTSTANDING
RESULTS
1975 + 1976

Lloyd super goal stuns Norwich

SO EASY, CITY

SKY BLUE QUICK VIEW

CITY STREAK IN!

CITY POWER ON

The gods

WILLIE CARR

THE DEADLY DUO FERGIE AND WALLY

Scots need Ian's power

BOOK 1

Coventry city football book

COVENTRY CITY F.C.

Book 1

Glue

NEIL RAMSBOTTOM IN HIS BOLTON DAYS

WILLIE CARR 1966-1978

ERNIE MACHIN WON F.A. TO THE F.A. CORD AND FUN

WILLIE CARR

FIRST DIVISION

IAN BUTTERWORTH Midfield. Born Crewe. Ht. 5.11. Wt. 11.5. Age 18. Was also given his first senior outing for the club in an F.A. Cup tie against Manchester City in January 1982 shortly before his 18th birthday. First League game in March 1982 against Swansea also as substitute. Originally signed as a schoolboy and later as apprentice, he turned professional in August 1981. In 1982-83 he added to his regular appearances and had completed 44 for the club by the end of it.

BOBBY GOULD
COVENTRY CITY Manager

BOBBY GOULD Manager. Took over towards the end of last season having been manager of Bristol Rovers previously. Formerly assistant manager at Aldershot and coach at Chelsea, he had had a distinguished career as a centre-forward with Coventry, Arsenal, Wolves, Bristol City, West Bromwich, West Ham, Bristol Rovers and Hereford, scoring 160 League goals. Also briefly with Wimbledon.

IAN BUTTERWORTH
COVENTRY CITY

NICK PLATNAUER Midfield. Born Bedford. Ht. 5.11. Wt. 12.10. Age 22. Was a close-season signing in 1983 by manager Bobby Gould from his former club Bristol Rovers. A midfield player who had enjoyed a successful first season with the west country club after being signed from Bedford Town. Signed in August 1982, he made his League debut in midfield against Lincoln the following month and finished the season on the 24 appearances mark with seven goals. Cost City £35,000 in a deal involving his colleague Graham Withey.

GERRY DALY
COVENTRY CITY

GERRY DALY Midfield. Born Dublin. Ht. 5.8. Wt. 11.4. Age 29. Experienced midfield player who joined Manchester United in April 1973 from the Republic of Ireland club Bohemians. League debut against Arsenal in August 1973 and moved to Derby County in March 1977. Transferred to Coventry in August 1980 for £310,000, he was loaned to Leicester for a spell during 1982-83. Had completed 296 League appearances during his career by the end of the season.

NICK PLATNAUER
COVENTRY CITY

GRAHAM WITHEY Forward. Born Bristol. Ht. 6.0. Wt. 11.12. Age 23. His first two appearances for Bristol Rovers last season were as substitute and in the second of them against Wigan in October he scored twice. Made 22 League appearances in all and scored ten goals in his first campaign in the League. Former tax inspector who was signed at a cost of £5,000 from Bath City in August 1982 and made his first appearance in the No. 12 shirt against Brentford in the same month. Signed with Nick Platnauer.

...ENNETT Forward. Born Manchester. Ht. 6.0. Age 24. Developed with his local club ...ter City, he turned professional with them in 978 and was given his first chance in the ...de as substitute against Everton in April 1979. ...ed to Cardiff City in September 1981 he became ...r choice in attack and last season scored 12 ...41 league appearances. Has a total of 129 ...appearances and 27 goals. Coventry signing in summer of 1983.

TERRY GIBSON
COVENTRY CITY

TERRY GIBSON Forward. Born London. Ht. 5.5. Wt. 10.0. Age 21. An England international at Schools and Youth level, he developed at White Hart Lane after his

PANINI

Panini's first set of domestic League cards came out under the Top Sellers name in 1972, but it wasn't until later in the 70s that they hit their stride, producing uniform, trusted sticker sets which were actually sticky.

Under this onslaught, A&BC lost their way and were bought out by the American firm Topps, who temporarily brought a little baseball card razamatazz and glam-rock style to proceedings. Still, the days of cardboard were numbered - as were those of good old FKS, who responded to the Panini steamroller with their own sticky set of bizarre gold stickers in 1978 before quietly biting the dust.

The Panini Revolution stood for reliability, professionalism, mass popularity and a return to hundreds of near-identical head shots, albeit with little flags and team crests.

It seemed that everyone had a copy of that debut *Football 78* album in their school bag, along with a pile of swaps held in place with a laggy band. Our new favourite thing was twice as hefty as its predecessor, weighing in at a fat 64 pages; each club spread over two pages instead of one, and in total there were 525 stickers to collect.

COVENTRY CITY

HIGHFIELD ROAD

COVENTRY CITY
BRIAN ROBERTS

COVENTRY CITY
PETER HORMANTSCHUK

COVENTRY CITY
IAN BUTTERWORTH

COVENTRY CITY
STEVE WHITTON

Midfield. Born East Ham. Ht. 6.0.

The stickers themselves were beautifully designed, clear head-and-shoulders shots with a club badge and a St George's or St Andrew's flag because, yes, the Scots had been included too. Clydebank's Billy McColl got to have his own sticker, and the English Second Division was also covered with a team group and badge for each previously ignored team.

Ah, those badges. There was a heartbeat jump when you ripped open your packet and saw a gold foil City badge nestling among the half-dozen stickers...

Panini reigned for a good fifteen years, never straying far from their '78 blueprint, producing a series of highly collectable and well-loved albums until they, in turn, were replaced by Merlin

around the time the Premier League was launched and the licensing fees leapt up.

The Panini Football 1991 sticker album proudly bore the crests of the Football League and the PFA together

Chairman: J.W.T. Hill
Secretary: J.D. Dent
Manager: Gordon Milne
Coach: Ron Wylie
Captain: Mick Coop
Year formed: 1883
Ground capacity: 48,000

FOOTBALL LEAGUE
FIRST DIVISION
COVENTRY CITY

Coventry City

Highfield Road

Chairman: Sir Jack Scamp, DL. JP
Manager: Gordon Milne
Secretary: Eddie Plumley
Coach: Ron Wiley
Captain: Terry Yorath
Year formed: 1883
Ground capacity: 48,000
Record attendance: 51,457 v Wolves, Division 2, April 1967
Honours: Division Two Champions: 1966-67
Division Three Champions: 1963-64
Division Three (South) Champions: 1935-36
Colours: All sky blue, with white & dark blue trim.
Change colours: All red with white & dark blue trim.

COVENTRY CITY

BRIAN ROBER

GORDON MILNE (M

JIM BLYTH

45

COVENTRY CITY

DAVE SEXTON Joined Coventry in the summer of 1981 after his quite unexpected dismissal by Manchester United. Dave was a player with Chelmsford, Luton, West Ham, Orient, Brighton and Palace, and managed Orient, Chelsea and Q.P.R. before moving to Old Trafford in June 1977. He is also looking after the England Under-21 team.

DAVE SEXTON
COVENTRY CITY Manager

GERRY DALY
COVENTRY CITY

... Ht. 5.9 Wt. 10.10 Age ... his career with Bohe-Manchester United, for ...nst Arsenal in August ...hem before moving to ... leading League scorer ...30 □ 10 (EI) ...

TOMMY ENGLISH
COVENTRY CITY

...Cirencester. Ht. 5.9 Wt. ...international who signed ...79 and made his League ...ing day of the 1979-80 ...ed up his 50th League ...March 1981, and finished ...west League scorer with

STEVE HUNT
COVENTRY CITY

...ngham. Ht. 5.7 Wt. 10.11 ...n Villa, but made only ...ing tempted to join New ...offer in the States, Steve ...First Division, and so in ...ce to join Coventry, for a ...t success, missing only

PETER BODAK
COVENTRY CITY

...ngham. Ht. 5.8 Wt. 9.10 ...club straight from school ...ional forms in May 1979. ...hile playing for the Birm-...Made his League debut ... 1980, and immediately ...where he is sure to be a

...am Birmingham. Ht. 6.0 ...youth international who ...th Coventry and signed ... 1977. His League debut ...and although his career ...g sustained in a training ...n and finished 1980-81 as ...s and Cups.

...Liverpool. Ht. 6.1 Wt. 11.7 ...national, Mark is the son ...avelled striker in his day ...gned on as an apprentice ...e grade as a professional ...ue debut against Wolves ...on, but really started to ...on.

with that of the Scottish League and pro body counterparts. What Panini didn't know was that Merlin (AKA good old Topps, if you read the small print) were waiting in the wings to scupper the comfy status quo with a deal already tied up with the brand-new Premier League.

In 1992, Panini's remaining PFA licence allowed them only to produce stickers of the players rather than any club details. How sad it was to see official stats replaced by weedy 'captain's comments' and it got worse when kits were no longer able to be shown – players trotted out in standard white PFA boiler suits – or else players' kit was recoloured in lairy greens, reds and oranges in the utterly emasculated 'Super Players From Top Teams' of '96.

While Panini responded by skittering down the leagues for material, Merlin's *Premier League 1994* debut featured PL badges, team groups, full info and players in kits, bright and beautiful. There was even a page for Sky TV cards.

THE SKY BLUES

PANINIS FOOTBALL 88

JOHN SILLETT
COVENTRY CITY

STEVE OGRIZOVIC
COVENTRY CITY

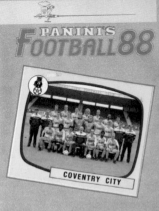

COVENTRY CITY

JOHN SILLETT Manager. Now that George Curtis has been made managing director, chief coach John Sillett has been put in charge of the team, though Curtis still gets involved in training sessions. Between them, they created a consistent team in 1986-87 and were rewarded by a marvellous win in the FA Cup final.

STEVE OGRIZOVIC Goalkeeper. Born Mansfield. Ht.6.3. Wt.15.0. Age 30. Steve didn't miss a single League game last season — for the fifth year in a row! Started his career with Chesterfield, and had spells with Liverpool and Shrewsbury before transferring to Coventry in June 1984. Career total of 230 League games.

46

TEAMS THAT YOU CAN RECITE

When teams were teams rather than private contractors of fleeting acquaintance, the first-choice line-up would go unchanged for seasons on end, with the boss blooding a kid or adding perhaps one new face over the close season, but only to replace the arthritic right-back who had just enjoyed his testimonial year.

You knew your team was a team because they piled into a team bath after the match, rather than wearing flip-flops and initialled dressing-gowns and insisting on private shower cubicles. You knew they were a team because their surnames seemed to rhyme when you recited them.

Glazier, Smith, Cattlin, Machin, Blockley, Barry, Mortimer, Carr, O'Rourke, Hunt, Parker...

What's the City team you can automatically recite?

Every year, you'd hear a news story about a fan who had named their firstborn after their whole beloved team.

Take a bow, William Wilfred Christopher Ernest Jeffrey Roy Dennis William John Stephen Robert Blenkinsop. You'll be coming up 43, next birthday. And, of course, it's now a family tradition to name a little one after your heroes, even though it doesn't really work so well in the era of huge League squads.

So spare a thought for poor little Lee Jordan Danny Andy Reda Conor John Josh Danny Jim Simeon Mohamed Shaun Billy Aaron Marcus Ryan Jordan Ryan Jack Ivor Reice James Blenkinsop.

'LoveLee' for short. Smashing little girl.

SKY BLUES

1 Bill GLAZIER
2 Mick COOP
3 Dietmar BRUCK
4 Mick KEARNS
5 Tony KNAPP
6 Brian HILL
7 Ronnie REES
8 Pat MORRISSEY
9 Bobby GOULD
10 Ernie MACHIN
11 David CLEMENTS
12 Brian LEWIS

SKY BLUES

1 BILL GLAZIER
2 MICK COOP
3 JIM HOLMES
4 DENNIS MORTIMER
5 JOHN CRAVEN
6 ALAN DUGDALE
7 WILLIE CARR
8 BRIAN ALDERSON
9 COLIN STEIN
10 ALAN GREEN
11 TOMMY HUTCHISON

TODAYS TEAMS

COVENTRY CITY		ASTON VILLA
Steve Ogrizovic	1	Nigel Spink
Brian Borrows	2	David Norton
Greg Downs	3	Tony Dorigo
Lloyd McGrath	4	Allan Evans
Brian Kilcline	5	Paul Elliott
Trevor Peake	6	Martin Keown
Dave Bennett	7	Paul Birch
Dave Phillips	8	Simon Stainrod
Cyrille Regis	9	Garry Thompson
Micky Adams	10	Steve Hodge
Nick Pickering	11	Steve Hunt

47

Best Wishes
Trevor Peake

THE AUTOGRAPH BOOK

Gone out of existence. Withdrawn from the field. Abandoned. Missed. Passed by.

Everything we come across on this journey through the Lost World of Coventry City is no more. They thought it was all over – and they were dead right.

The autograph book was unlike any other of its day. Its cartridge-paper pages were blank, devoid of words and lines, with the built-in compensation of alternate pastel shades – chalky blue, green, pink, yellow. The outer corners of the pages were missing, rounded off so as not to offend the hand of an honoured victim. The spine of the leather-bound booklet ran down the short side, so it lolled open invitingly. On the cover of the book there was no author's name or title, just a single, golden word in a curly typeface. And then there was the vital loop of elastic to hold the book closed in the owner's back pocket, either encircling the whole precious volume, or just stretching over a single corner.

Lost. Let slip. No longer in our possession.

It isn't just the autograph book that has bitten the dust in recent years, but also the crowd of small boys hanging around the locked double door marked PLAYERS AND OFFICIALS ONLY an hour after the match. The players are missing, too: men who didn't need a minder at their side to talk to a twelve-year-old about the afternoon's brawls and cannonballs. The kind of players whose personally signed message you'd want to treasure forever. Micky Adams. Trevor Peake. Perry Suckling…

The warning signs came when first two, then three, and now four of the five attackers in every team were phased out, goalscoring deemed surplus to requirement. Local heroes fell out of fashion. Red-faced stoppers failed to evolve with changing times, and so soon became extinct. And the best player in every team of the Sixties and Seventies became the first called up to the great kickaround in the sky.

All gone, but not forgotten.

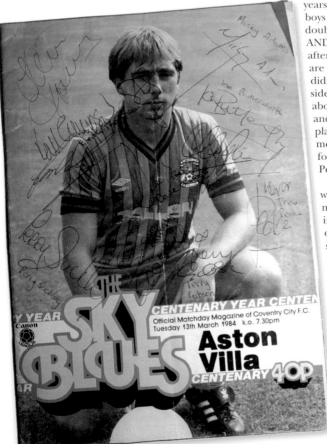

THE SKY BLUES
Official Matchday Magazine of Coventry City F.C.
Tuesday 13th March 1984 k.o. 7.30pm
CENTENARY YEAR CENTEN
Aston Villa
CENTENARY 40P
Canon

Not a Lot of People Know That: When Tallon were first announced as sponsors, City were handily wearing the old 'T for Talbot' kit.

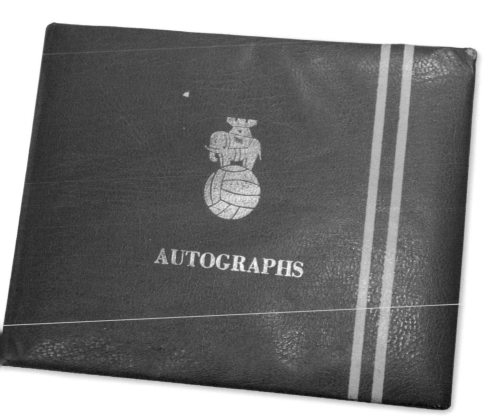

The kind of players whose message you'd want to treasure forever.

Micky Adams. Trevor Peake. Perry Suckling...

Then as now, football magazines and club shops churned out sheets of pre-printed (quite literally auto-) autographs to help save the all-important stars time and hassle. It's all a question of supply and demand, see? But it's odd how much more charming the old sheets seem in comparison to today's handily pre-signed official postcards.

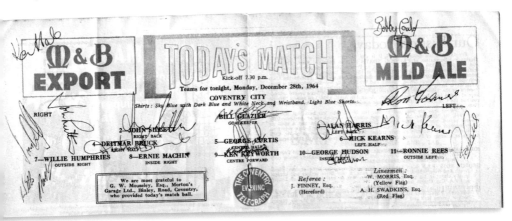

3

SUBBUTEO

Subbuteo was by far the most popular table-top representation of football, and its '00'-scale figures still hold a special place in the hearts of blokes across the globe. Part of the game's appeal was due to the huge range of accessories which, while unnecessary for the actual playing of the game, did prop up an illusion of realism and 'add to the big-match atmosphere'.

Plastic pitches were one of the ugliest developments in Eighties football. QPR, Luton and Oldham became unbeatable at home because they mastered the art of playing on a surface that had all the properties of lino – sliding tackles were out, except for players wearing motorcycle leathers under their shorts. Meanwhile, good old Subbuteo exhibited their usual dogged determination to keep up with the times, producing their own 'Astroturf' pitch – although, if their 'grass' pitch was made of green baize cloth, and the 'Astroturf' surface from

The 'Heavyweight' figures of the Seventies had a stance that suggested they were
well up for it.

slightly different baize cloth, it's unclear in what sense it was any more 'artificial'.

The rampant hooliganism of the time puts into stark perspective any complaints about plastic pitches, leading as it did to football attendances going down and spike-topped fences going up. Subbuteo didn't shirk its remit to mirroring the game and replaced its friendly green picket fences with prison railings and mounted police to keep any potential plastic yobboes off the pitch.

The actual Subbuteo playing figures of the late Sixties to late Seventies are known these days as Heavyweights, with their National

4   5   6   14

Service haircuts, big claret-topped socks and a stance that suggested they were well up for it.

The Seventies also saw short-lived and unloved 'Scarecrows' and 'Zombies' figures (sporting the all-blue Umbro kits); before the Eighties brought the more detailed, and more popular, 'Lightweights' which endured to the mid-Nineties 'Pony' era.

Although accessories such as the dugouts and the ambulance men, the TV tower with mini-Motty, the floodlights and VIP figures (including Queenie handing over a tiny FA Cup) were affordable and always welcome on a Christmas morning, the ultimate prize had to be the Subbuteo stadium, complete with a decent crowd of ready-painted spectators. Unfortunately, they were beyond the pocket of most kids' parents and you'd count yourself lucky to have a single, foot-long stand with a couple of dozen spectators dotted around it.

We used to buy packs of unpainted spectators – fifty per box, all as naked as the day they were moulded – and only after weeks of eye-damaging work on Polo-Neck Man, Fatty, Celebrating Man and his equally Celebrating Girlfriend, did we discover the ultimate

irony: with stands on all four sides it was virtually impossible to play the game without nudging a stand and causing a mini-stadium disaster.

Oh, come on, let's go up the park and play football.

14

4

59

74   **51**

COMIC CUTS

In all your adult life, have you ever known anything quite as exciting as when a Sky Blues teamgroup appeared in *Shoot!* – or when City were featured in one of the other regular rotating comic spots such as *Scorcher*'s 'When the Crowd Roared'? And, cooyer, how about when it promised 'Coventry City could challenge for the honours next season'..?

Such earth-shaking events could easily even eclipse the longed-for weekly instalment of your comic heroes' stories.

Were you a Roy of the Rovers kid? Not every Coventry fan went in for the

Were you a Roy of the Rovers kid?
Or one for the plucky underdogs?

Who goes there? Can you name these City stars... without peeking at the text?

world-beating supermen, preferring instead the plucky underdogs such as 'Nipper' and Billy Dane and his magic boots in *Scorcher*, the *Valiant*'s 'Raven

NOEL CANTWELL WAS MANAGER OF THE SKY BLUES WHEN THEY WERE FEATURED IN 1968!

On The Wing' or 'The Boy in the Velvet Mask' out of *Roy of the Rovers* comic.

My personal all-time favourite was *Scorcher*'s 'The Kangaroo Kid', who was brilliant and heartbreakingly rubbish in just the right proportions...

Second Division Redstone Rovers were on a pre-season tour of Australia when they spotted a feral teen frolicking with a flock of kangaroos in the outback. When he clocked the half-naked wildman's party tricks with a stray practice ball, manager Barney Patch had only one thought: Secret Weapon.

The Kid's League debut: a voice in the crowd: "Gah, the cross is too high. But wait, the wild-haired substitute is leaping to head it. No... to *volley* it into the net..."

The Kid raises a powerful forepaw and punches the sky. Kangaroo buddies Tarkil and Darga go ape in the dugout.

Raised as a marsupial in a pouchful of regular joeys, yet destined to take the steps of Wembley in a single bounce. Now that's what I call rags to riches.

THE ALL·SOCCER PAPER THAT'S TOP OF THE LEAGUE!

Scorcher and SCORE 4p

EVERY MONDAY   **1st JULY, 1972**

TOP TEAMS
COVENTRY CITY

[Y]RS AGO THE COVENTRY [N]EARLY ALL RODE TO THEIR [ ]BIKES ! THEY WORKED AT [CY]CLE FACTORY AND [ ]THE WORKS TEAM. THEY [ ]EIR NAME TO COVENTRY [ ]. BUT DID NOT JOIN THE [LE]AGUE DIVISION R]UNTIL [ ]S NEVER VERY BRIGHT [ ]EVERAL UPS AND DOWNS [ ]ROPPED INTO THE FOURTH [ ]50

WITHIN ONE SEASON THEY RETURNED TO THE THIRD DIVISION. IT WAS THE START OF AN AMAZING PERIOD IN THE CLUB'S HISTORY. JIMMY HILL (ABOVE RIGHT), WAS APPOINTED MANAGER AND THE NEW SKY BLUES BEGAN TO HIT THE HEADLINES. THEY WERE THIRD DIVISION CHAMPIONS IN 1964 AND WITHIN THREE YEARS THEY WERE IN THE FIRST DIVISION. THE CAPTAIN OF THE SIDE THROUGH- OUT THAT WONDERFUL RUN OF SUCCESS WAS GIANT GEORGE CURTIS (LEFT), NOW WITH ASTON VILLA.

BUT WITH THEIR MANY YOUNG PLAYING STARS—MEN LIKE WILLIE CARR (RIGHT), JEFF BLOCKLEY, BOBBY PARKER, MICK McGUIRE AND DENNIS MORTIMER — TOGETHER WITH BOBBY GRAHAM, £70,000 CAPTURE FROM LIVERPOOL, COVENTRY CITY COULD CHALLENGE FOR THE HONOURS NEXT SEASON.

1972   Australia 15c., New Zealand 15c., South Africa 12c., Rhodesia 13c., West Africa 1/2d., Malaysia 60c., Malta 1/-d.

Grrrrrooveh: Tremendous swinging sock turnover alert!

53

COVENTRY

Back Row (L. to R.), David Cross, Tommy Hutchinson, Jim Blyth, Peter Hindley, Neil Ramsbottom, Chris Cattlin, Mick Ferguson, Dennis Mortimer, Larry Lloyd. Front Row (L. to R.), Alan Green, Alan Dugdale, John Craven, Ron Wylie (Team Coach), Gordon Milne (Team Manager), Graham Oakey, Mick Coop, Les Cartwright, Jim Holmes.

K CARR Coventry City and Scotland

THE BEDROOM SHRINE

You can rebuild it, y'know – the bedroom shrine of your youth when you loved them all, even the dodgy old full-back on whom the adults would pour scorn and derision.

From a time when you wanted to see their images last thing at night and first thing in the morning; arranged in teamgroup ranks, watching over you while you slept.

The thrill of opening a *Goal*, or *Shoot!* or *Tiger* and seeing a real actual City star featured on a colour poster – or, even better, a team photo in the centre spread – might not be so keen now. But don't let that hold you back.

You can still get the horrible woodchip wallpaper we all had in our bedrooms, and paint it that turquoise light blue that was in vogue in the mid-Seventies. Someone will still have the recipe.

And there are people on eBay who make it their business to go through old magazines and annuals pulling out the posters of your club, flogging them by the dozen. The collection that took you seven years to accrue can now be obtained in a couple of days.

It won't have organically spread across your wall over the years like a fungus of devotion, but it will still look magnificent.

Almost certainly, the wife will understand.

DENNIS MORTIMER
Coventry City

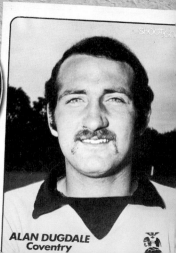

ALAN DUGDALE
Coventry

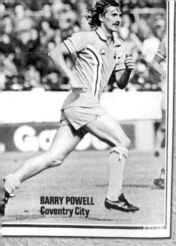

BARRY POWELL
Coventry City

TEAM SETS | **COVENTRY**

DAVE CLEMENTS   JEFF BLOCKLEY   WILLIE CARR

MICK COOP   NEIL MARTIN   BILL GLAZIER

START NOW! COLLECT THE WHOLE SERIES!

GLAZIER

COVENTRY CITY

FIRST TEAM POOL

FRONT ROW : Ernie Machin, Chris Cattlin, Roy Barry, Noel Cantwell, Neil Martin, David Clements, Willie C...
MIDDLE ROW : Dennis Mortimer, Brian Hill, Bill Glazier, Brian Joicey, Eric McManus, Billy Rafferty, Jeff Blo...
BACK ROW : John O'Rourke, Bob Parker, Mick Coop, Tommy Gould, Ernie Hunt, Dietmar Bruck, ...Jeff Charl...

Bobby
McDonald
COVENTRY
CITY

101 JOHN BECK

55

Testimonial Match

THE TESTIMONIAL MATCH

When was the last time you went along to pay your respects to a great old servant of your club, putting up with the prospect of a meaningless friendly against local rivals – it's never quite the same, on their days off – in order to chip in to the loyal clubman's retirement nest egg as he looked forward to living in temporarily reduced circumstances and having to get a proper job? Eh?

There's no such thing as a testimonial match any more. Lining the pockets of a bloke who's far better off than yourself with the proceeds of a kickaround against a team with the suffix 'XI' doesn't count. The vital elements of long service, need, mutual gratitude and respect are all sadly absent.

Long service, need, mutual gratitude and respect...

Oggy Oggy Oggy: Holds City's record with 601 appearances in all competitions.

HARRY'S GAME

MONDAY 10th SEPTEMBER 1984
K.O. 7.30 p.m.
HIGHFIELD ROAD, COVENTRY
COV. CITY PAST XI v. COV. CITY PRESENT

DIETMAR BRUCK TESTIMONIAL MATCH

Highfield Road Stadium
COVENTRY
(by kind permission of the Directors
Coventry City F.C.)

WEDNESDAY, 26th APRIL 1972

EX COVENTRY CITY XI
v
JIMMY HILL'S INTERNATIONAL XI
(kick-off 7 p.m.)

COVENTRY CITY v CHARLTON ATHLETIC
(kick-off 8 p.m.)

Personal appearance of TOM COYNE
B.B.C. 'MIDLANDS TODAY'

plus other star attractions, including
PENALTY COMPETITION

SOUVENIR PROGRAMME 10p

| SKY BLUES v AS

The ERNIE MACHIN Testimonial

Highfield Road
Coventry
Tuesday
May 1st, 1973

10p
Official
Souvenir
Programme

Teams for
tonight's
games on
back page

Did You Know? After 11 years of loyal service, Bill Glazier moved on to Brentford in 1975.

BRIAN HILL
Testimonial Game

OFFICIAL
PROGRAMME 1/-

COVENTRY CITY TONY HATELEY
versus
DERBY COUNTY
JOHN O'HARE
at
HIGHFIELD ROAD
MONDAY 28th APRIL 1969

Our Bill'

The
BILL GLAZIER
TESTIMONIAL
Highfield Road
Coventry
Tuesday
November 26th
1974

OFFICIAL
SOUVENIR
PROGRAMME
10p

SKY BLUES
v
ENGLAND
1966
WORLD
CUP
XI

WE ALL SCREAM FOR ICE CREAM

We're guessing the ice cream industry hasn't had a great time of it recently, given the drizzly nature of our rather rubbish summers (notlikewhenwewerekids). Well, maybe they should start giving football badges away with their ice cream, like they did in 1971. That would soon have us running to the end of the street every time we heard the chimes playing 'The Whistler and his Dog'.

Mister Softee issued their '1st Division Football League Club Badges' for the 1971/72 season, featuring the 22 top-flight clubs plus England and Wales... but not Scotland where, presumably, it's a bit chilly for ice-cream and lollies.

Rarer editions of this set, which was issued for one more season, were branded 'Lord Neilson' and 'Tonibell'.

Was it just our dads that said: "You know when the chimes are going? That means they've run out of ice cream"?

"Y'know when the chimes are going?

That means they've run out of ice-cream."

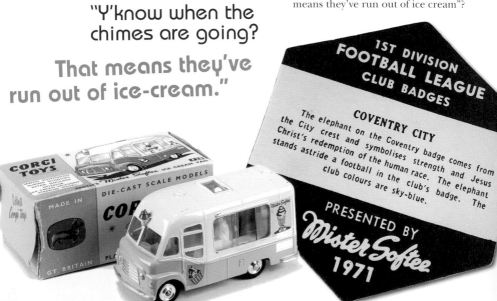

1ST DIVISION
FOOTBALL LEAGUE
CLUB BADGES

COVENTRY CITY

The elephant on the Coventry badge comes from the City crest and symbolises strength and Jesus Christ's redemption of the human race. The elephant stands astride a football in the club's badge. The club colours are sky-blue.

PRESENTED BY
Mister Softee
1971

RIBERO

Founded in 1988, little known sportswear firm Ribero landed the kit contract for Coventry City in time for the Premier League's inaugural season in 1992/93, but most City fans weren't too impressed with the rather involved design.

It came hot on the trail of two other kits that were controversial in their own way, the Hummel 'test card' kit which saw the beloved Cup Final strip by Triple S ditched after just one season; and then the Asics kit which sought to return, too late, to the Cup-winning style.

Most often desribed frankly as 'the birdshit kit', the Ribero wasn't particularly popular, though nowadays all the kits from this era are known to go for silly money on eBay.

It's pictured here on the programme cover in a game against Norwich, who wore the yellow-and-green version of the same kit. At least they had a polite name for it in Norfolk: 'scrambled egg and parsley'…

FOCUS ON...

Back in the 70s, Coventry City's Robert Parker lay to shame every modern footballer who ever filled in a programme questionnaire namedropping property portfolios and £750 cocktails. Bobby didn't like bad refs or conceited people, but he was partial to records and clothes, a nice bit of steak and Holland. Bobby didn't drive a car, but you can picture him getting dressed up and walking round to one of his many close friends' houses to spin some Temptations or Supremes records, maybe to watch *Top of the Pops* on a Thursday night. That's when he'd speak modestly of his dream of playing for England, or possibly being a draughtsman in another life.

Wee (5ft 6ins) William Carr tells it like it is. Or rather was. **FAVOURITE FOOD:** Roast beef 'n' Yorkshire pudding. **FAVOURITE SINGERS:** Andy Williams, Diana Ross. **CAR:** Volkswagen Valiant.

Willie doesn't like being late or overnight stops, but at least he'd been to the West Indies. He seems a contented soul, playing with his kids and going for a spin in his motor, practising so he was never late. **WHICH PERSON IN THE WORLD WOULD YOU MOST LIKE TO MEET?** Muhammad Ali; but just keep him away from **MOST DIFFICULT OPPONENT:** Any close markers.

Seeing as they both shared the hobbies of driving and golf, Willie and John Craven would have formed a natural golf-club two-ball. A three-ball, if one of them had offered to pick Bobby up.

Former Yoker Athletic and Dumbarton striker Ian Andrew Wallace was from Glasgow, and a man of the world. His **FAVOURITE FOOD** was cosmopolitan king prawn and fried rice; **BEST COUNTRY VISITED** was France and **IF YOU WEREN'T**

FOCUS ON

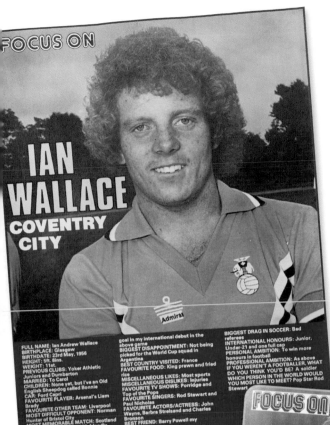

IAN WALLACE
COVENTRY CITY

Admiral

FULL NAME: Ian Andrew Wallace
BIRTHPLACE: Glasgow
BIRTHDATE: 23rd May, 1956
HEIGHT: 5ft. 8ins.
WEIGHT: 11st.
PREVIOUS CLUBS: Yoker Athletic Juniors and Dumbarton
MARRIED: To Carol
CHILDREN: None yet, but I've an Old English Sheepdog called Bonnie
CAR: Ford Capri
FAVOURITE PLAYER: Arsenal's Liam Brady
FAVOURITE OTHER TEAM: Liverpool
MOST DIFFICULT OPPONENT: Norman Hunter of Bristol City
MOST MEMORABLE MATCH: Scotland v. Bulgaria, February, 1978, friendly
BIGGEST THRILL: Scoring the winning goal in my international debut in the above game
BIGGEST DISAPPOINTMENT: Not being picked for the World Cup squad in Argentina
BEST COUNTRY VISITED: France
FAVOURITE FOOD: King prawn and fried rice
MISCELLANEOUS LIKES: Most sports
MISCELLANEOUS DISLIKES: Injuries
FAVOURITE TV SHOWS: Porridge and Top of the Pops
FAVOURITE SINGERS: Rod Stewart and Paul Nicholas
FAVOURITE ACTORS/ACTRESS: John Wayne, Barbra Streisand and Charles Bronson
BEST FRIEND: Barry Powell my team-mate
BIGGEST DRAG IN SOCCER: Bad referees
INTERNATIONAL HONOURS: Junior, Under-21 and one full cap
PERSONAL AMBITION: To win more honours in football
PROFESSIONAL AMBITION: As above
IF YOU WEREN'T A FOOTBALLER, WHAT DO YOU THINK YOU'D BE? A soldier
WHICH PERSON IN THE WORLD WOULD YOU MOST LIKE TO MEET? Pop Star Rod Stewart

Chicken in a basket, gym teacher, Raquel Welch and Benny Hill.

A PROFESSIONAL FOOTBALLER, WHAT DO YOU THINK YOU'D BE: A soldier. See the world. Meet exotic people. You know the routine.

Meanwhile, in 1973, left-back Chris Cattlin admitted he was yet another Motown man, his fave singers being Marvin Gaye, Dionne Warwick and… Harry Secombe. Chris also liked learning other people's customs and football techniques; he watched *Horizon* and *Dave Allen at Large*, and wanted to one day write a novel.

FOCUS ON

JOHN CRAVEN
Coventry

FULL NAME: John Roland Craven
BIRTHPLACE: St. Annes-on-Sea, Lancs.
BIRTHDATE: May 15th, 1947
HEIGHT: 5ft 11½ins.
WEIGHT: 13st 8lbs
PREVIOUS CLUBS: Blackpool, Crystal Palace
MARRIED: Yes, to Christine
CHILDREN: Mark (2½) and Lee (4 months)
CAR: MGB GT
FAVOURITE PLAYER: Colin Todd
FAVOURITE OTHER TEAM: Liverpool
MOST DIFFICULT OPPONENT: Denis Law
MOST MEMORABLE MATCH: My League debut against Spurs
BIGGEST THRILL: My four goals against Leeds and Arsenal last season (with Palace)
BIGGEST DISAPPOINTMENT: Blackpool's relegation to Division Two
BEST COUNTRY VISITED: Canada
FAVOURITE FOOD: Italian
MISCELLANEOUS LIKES: Golf, reading, driving
MISCELLANEOUS DISLIKES: Sundays, hooliganism on the terraces
FAVOURITE T.V. SHOWS: Morecambe and Wise, Colombo
FAVOURITE SINGERS: Glen Campbell, Neil Diamond
FAVOURITE ACTORS: Jack Lemmon, Alec Guinness
BEST FRIEND: John Jackson (Orient and ex Crystal Palace)
BIGGEST INFLUENCE ON CAREER: Stan Mortensen and Bob Stokoe, my Managers at Blackpool
BIGGEST DRAG IN SOCCER: 1 o'clock at 2.60 every Saturday
INTERNATIONAL HONOURS: None
PERSONAL AMBITION: Successful and happy life
PROFESSIONAL AMBITION: To play at Wembley
IF YOU WEREN'T A FOOTBALLER WHAT DO YOU THINK YOU'D BE? I don't know
WHICH PERSON IN THE WORLD WOULD YOU MOST LIKE TO MEET? Golfer Jack Nicklaus

MARSHALL CAVENDISH FOOTBALL HANDBOOK

Long before the age of YouTube or even the ubiquitous video recorder, there was no easy way to replay golden goals from the past – you just had to wait for them to be reshown on *Football Focus*, which could often prove quite a lengthy wait if you were waiting for a specific goal.

For most fans, there was some respite available thanks to the *Marshall Cavendish Football Handbook* ("in 873 weekly parts") and their smashing arrow- and dot-laded diagrams which traced the build-up to a goal in stunning time-lapse ImaginationVision – complete with added slight confusion, as players appeared two or three times as they ran through the action-packed scene.

The other main attraction of the *Handbook* was always the skill tips, direct from the finest football brains the League had to offer.

The Marshall Cavendish Coventry City collection ensured any mustard-keen soccer kid could kick any ball with any part of his clodhopper. First Mick Co-Op demonstrated in stop-action stills how to control a ball with the inside of your foot; then Ian Wallace trotted across the page in multiple frames, slicing the ball high and wide of the right-hand upright in the name of exclusive one-on-one coaching.

The Marshall Cavendish Coventry City collection
ensured any soccer kid could kick any ball with any part of his clodhopper.

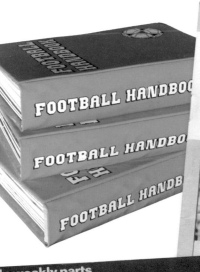

FOOTBALL HANDBOOK
FOOTBALL HANDBOOK
FOOTBALL HANDBOOK

In weekly parts
30p   THE MARSHALL CAVENDISH

PART 15

FOOTBALL HANDBOOK

FACTS & FIGURES·PRIZE QUIZ.

In weekly parts
30p   THE MARSHALL CAVENDISH

PART 38

FOOTBALL HANDBOOK

IAN WALLACE
Outside help

PETER SHILTON
Super saver

KEVIN REEVES
Norwich new boy

DAVID MILLS
£500,000 Baggie

ALLY McLEOD
Following up

FEATURES·MATCH ACTION·FACTS & FIGURES·QUIZ

Chocolate-brown tramlines: Unbelievably, this iconic kit is regularly voted as Britain's worst ever!

SCARF ACE

For many fans of a certain age, the 'new-fangled' silk scarves with built-in text never really hit the spot as satisfyingly as the good old blue-and-white 'bar scarves' knitted by your nanna.

Back in the olden days, 'knitting' was a kind of folk art which enabled nice

'Knitting' was a folk art
whereby old ladies fashioned football scarve
direct from sheep's bottoms.

old ladies to fashion baby clothes and football scarves direct from the wool that grew naturally on sheep's bottoms. Magical, in retrospect.

It's the sensual memory of a snug woollen scarf pulled up around your face in winter that lingers – along with the slightly soggy sensation of pulling your scarf back in through the crack in the car window when you were travelling away with all colours blazing.

But to a whole new 70s generation, the groovy silk scarf was where it was at.

Even today, I recall the exact moment I was first stopped in my tracks by a 'look'. I was sat on the front wall of the Kop when this style apparition wandered past: hair short on top with a hint of centre parting, but long at the back and sides; huge pin-striped flares with two rows of buttons on the thick waistband; tan Doc Martens; a tight-fitting denim jacket over a big-collared shirt and, the pièce de résistance, a silk* scarf tied round his wrist.

Available for 60p from the club shop, my scarf was pricey but worth every penny. When it wasn't pinned to my wall as part of my shrine it was round my wrist – not just on match days, but around the house all week.

Now, how to persuade Mam to get me some bovver boots?

...RE MAGIC

COVENTRY

Sky Reds at Night: Anyone out there remember City's red and blue change strip circa 1975/76?

The pièce de résistance, **a silk* scarf** tied round the wrist.

* 100% Polyester

TOPICAL TIMES

Always a welcome addition to a Christmas morning pillowcase, the *Topical Times Football Book* kept young football fans entertained from the late 1950s to just beyond the millennium. A full set of the books would now form an important historical document, charting social progress through the second half of the 20th century. The players featured in the plentiful and lavish colour photos, both on and off the field, start out as Brylcreemed wage slaves, then move through their bushy-haired, flared phase looking like they've got a few quid to spend, before unexpectedly ending up as genuine millionaires.

The Topical Times

FOOTBALL

BOOK 1992

PEUGEOT

Candy

INSIDE –
pages
packed with

BIG NAME
INTERVIEWS

COLOUR
PIN-UPS

ACTION
PIC

Not the most topical of 1960s newspapers, having gone under in the '40s...

The *Topical Times* was once a popular weekly paper for kids, with cartoon strips mainly devoted to football, running almost precisely between the wars – from 1919 to 1940. It was perhaps best known for its glossy football cards given away in sets of three, which feelgood factor prompted DC Thomson, publishers of *The Beano* and *Dandy*, to retain the name when they launched their new annuals.

The presentation was lively in design, picture led, and featured a seemingly never-ending supply of different fonts. A much-favoured device was to introduce a tenuous link to a set of photos, with players in curious poses always popular.

As well as punchy headlines, the stories had a hint of the tabloid about them, and the 'Their Other Team' spread enabled us to spy on stars relaxing at home in suburbia with the wife and kids amid flock wallpaper and velour sofas. Jealous, us?

ERNIE HUNT, Coventry City

THE RATTLE

The other day, I wandered down to the football from the pub and took my seat at one minute to kick-off, as usual, in order to avoid any kind of 'match-experience' shenanigans. Before I could sit down I had to extricate an object from the laggy band that secured it to my seat. It was a folded sheet of laminated card in club colours, called a 'clap-banner', which explained the horrendous noise that had assaulted my eardrums since I'd entered the ground.

Needless to say, I immediately took against it.

But when the frenzied clacking had died down a bit, I did at least concede that my age was partly to blame. For I once received a football rattle for my birthday that made a quite spectacular noise when I whizzed it round my head. So much so, that its use had to be rationed in the house.

One (young) person's great sound is another (old) person's unholy racket. That explains why the vuvuzela all but ruined the 2010 World Cup for me (along with England's risible performance), while some people thought they were such splendid fun, they started to take them to League games the following season.

The football rattle enjoyed its heyday in the 1960s, when they became as iconic a symbol of football-supporterdom as the scarf and bobble-hat.

They were nearly always homemade, employing the sort of engineering skills that only Dad could manage, and painted up in glossy club colours with the team name added as a finishing touch.

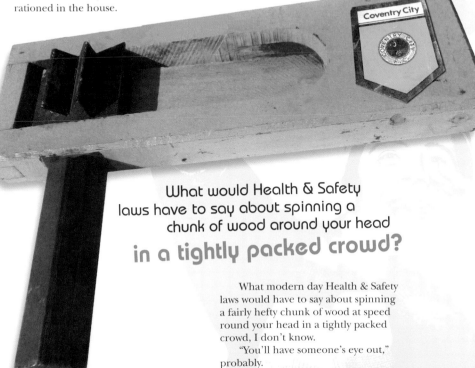

What would Health & Safety laws have to say about spinning a chunk of wood around your head in a tightly packed crowd?

What modern day Health & Safety laws would have to say about spinning a fairly hefty chunk of wood at speed round your head in a tightly packed crowd, I don't know.

"You'll have someone's eye out," probably.

SHOOT!

Allowed one comic a week, I'd already graduated from the entry-level *Beano* to *Scorcher*, but not until the summer of 1974, while immersed in the West Germany World Cup, did I consider myself man enough to step up to *Shoot!*

Eight pence was the price of admission, and I was soon in beyond the full-colour cover of Billy Bremner playing for Scotland against Brazil.

Now I could dive headlong into an article by Bobby Moore – every week, he'd let us backstage, behind the scenes in the life of a living, breathing football hero – and what's more I could puzzle over the fiendish problems posed in 'You Are the Ref'; study up-close World Cup action featuring Australia, Scotland, Holland, Zaire, DDR and Yugoslavia; chortle at the 'Football Funnies'; 'Focus On' Paul Gilchrist of Southampton (Miscellaneous Likes: motor racing, oil painting, music), and realise there were people just like me all over the country,

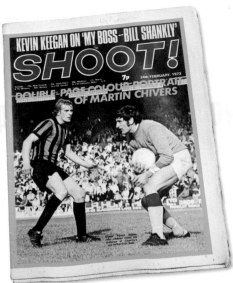

COLOUR ACTION OF PELE – IN ENGLAND!

SHOOT!

7p

28th APRIL, 1973

courtesy of the 'Goal Lines' letters page and 'Ask the Expert' readers' queries.

If I was lucky, there'd be a full-page star poster to add to my shrine, though this only happened once in a blue moon. It's difficult to explain now how a photo could be so prized, Blu-Tacked instantly up on your wall, but in the days of black newsprint papers and monochrome TV, the eight colour pages in *Shoot!* were like oases in a grey desert.

For five years my collection grew, filling several boxes, until 1979 when my head was finally turned by an attractive newcomer called *Match Weekly*.

I'm sorry I dropped you, *Shoot!*, and I'm even sorrier that we now live in a world where kids can't leg it down to the newsagents to eagerly pore over the latest issue.

Gabby:
Vociferous Terry Yorath captained City to seventh spot in 1977/78.

IN COLOUR SCOTLAND'S SOUTH AMERICAN TOUR

SHOOT!

15p

6th AUGUST, 1977

'Top of the bill' Liverpool Players

TERRY YORATH
(Coventry City)

Scottish League fixtures for 1977-78

ALL THE SCOTTISH LEAGUE SCORERS 1978/79

MOBIL BADGES

We love these silk badges given away with Mobil petrol in the early 80s. When was the last time you visited a petrol station to be gifted a football collectable that you thought was worth holding on to for 30 years, fer chrissakes?

Made of pure 100% silk from a silkworm's bottom * and, as such, suitable for stitching on to your Sunday best anorak or parka?

Free with four gallons of 4-star.

The only downside, associated more with the free giveaway poster than the patches themselves, was the prospect of a giant Alan Hudson marauding down the country like King Kong or Godzilla or worse – Dribble of Destruction Horror Shock – stomping down his non-shooting boot worryingly close to the vicinity of our beloved capital city.

Or possibly some kind of cheap polyester.

'T' FOR TALBOT

The great football innovator Jimmy Hill was always pushing and prodding at the boundaries of the game as we knew it. As part of his Sky Blue Revolution, he introduced one of Britain's first 'continental-style' one-colour kits in 1962.

But in 1980 Hill pushed the envelope a little too far. Having hit upon the idea of sponsorship from local business partners, he planned to rename the club 'Coventry Talbot' and even sneaked a red 'T' badge onto the shirt. The FA blocked the name change, but couldn't find anything in the rules to prevent Cov taking to the field in an outlandish new kit for 1981/82 with a huge Talbot 'T' logo intrinsic to the design.

TV companies, however, refused to televise the Sky Blues in their blatant new 'Talbot Sports' strip. Eventually a compromise was reached where Coventry wore an odd-looking plain kit whenever they played in a televised game.

Thirty years on the English game is still holding out against corporate rechristenings, the last Talbot Horizon has long since rolled off the production line; and every club has a horrible all-seater stadium. Some you win, some you lose.

The 'Big T' kit followed one with a smaller red 'T' badge. The TV alternative had no 'T' at all!

ON THE MOVE WITH

⊕TALBOT

MILNE TIME

We asked the great Gordon Milne, Sky Blues coach and then boss during the 70s, about his time with Coventry City.

For starters, having played under Bill Shankly as a boss, did he later find himself doing Shanks-style things as a manager?

"Yes," Gordon admitted. "I don't think you'd gain much from just impersonating him, telling his stories or whatever, but I think that almost sub-consciously you learn how you worked and how you trained and how you prepared. I was very lucky with managers. I served about six and a half years under Shanks. I learnt a lot from my Dad, who was a manager as well. And with England I played under Alf Ramsey who was a completely different character. Then I worked with Joe Mercer at Coventry, so I undoubtedly had a good education.

GNG: How would you describe your own style of management?

GM: I'm certainly not a tea cup thrower. I did my work during the week, I liked to be out there on the pitch when I could. I tried to get a collective team spirit going and I liked players to balance each other so that they felt comfortable in what they were doing. I liked to put square pegs in square holes. Without me shouting and screaming, I think they knew when to toe the line and when they could get away with a bit. I wanted my players to believe in what we were doing.

GNG: How did things start out at Highfield Road?

GM: When I first went to Coventry there was a bit of a heavy mob there, Willie Carr, Roy Barry, Ernie Hunt… a lot of old soldiers that had to be sorted out!

GNG: Was it frustrating being the manager of what was undoubtedly a selling club at that time?

GM: At Coventry we were producing a lot of good young players and every year we were losing one. But that was the nature of the business then. I had Jimmy Hill as chairman then and I think he was one of the best chairmen you could ever hope to work for. He would say to me in the summer: "Look, this is what we're doing, it might affect the team, but this is what we're doing." In a way that was him admitting that it was hard for me to lose good players and keep coming up with the results which took a little bit of pressure off from above.

GNG: How did the end come about at Coventry?

GM: I had nine years as manager there and then I had a year upstairs when Dave Sexton came. Although he is actually older than me it was like the young coach coming in who doesn't want to be concerned with contracts and stuff. Dave just wanted to be out there and he would even take a full session with the kids, he was good like that. Anyway, I did it for a year but I didn't really enjoy it. I was too young to do that role and I thought this is me getting farmed out here. I wasn't ready for that.

GNG: Give us an example of your type of player…

GM: I remember Ronnie Allen at Coventry saying: "You've got to give the fans hope." Big Tommy Hutchison was the sort of player who did that. He would beat four players then decide not to cross it, then lose it, then get it back and beat four again. It must have been frustrating for the strikers who played with him, but the fans loved him.

I still think that is true to this day. As a fan going to the game, you have to have somebody that you like to watch, especially if the team aren't too good. Someone who can do something to make your trip worthwhile…"

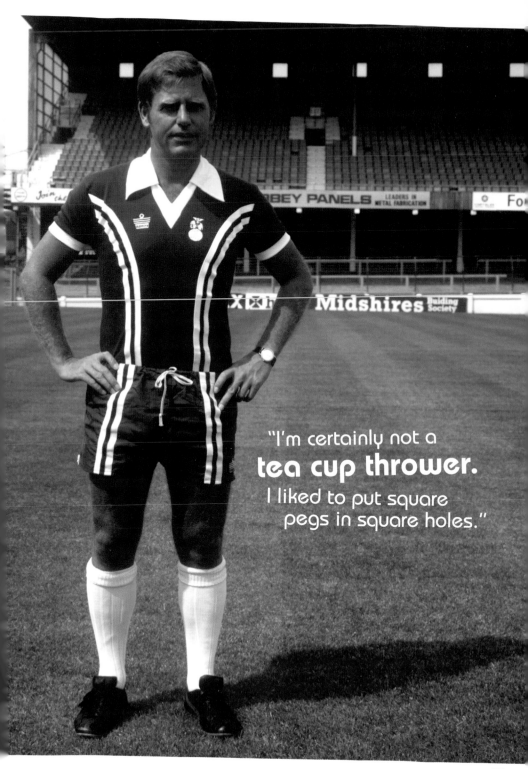

"I'm certainly not a
tea cup thrower.
I liked to put square
pegs in square holes."

WHAT A SHOT

For anyone who's just let out a big nostalgic sigh at the sight of these snapshots featuring the backs of fans' heads, distant players and pitches taken through spiky-topped perimeter fences, we've got plenty more where these came from!

Thanks go out to our number one Cov contributor Dean Gordon for these Polaroid humdingers from the post-Cup Final bus tour and the subsequent comedown on City's return to Wembley for the Charity Shield – all snapped from the terraces and the tour route in the belief that the results would prove worthy of the back page when they arrived back from the developers.

If you feel the need to gaze upon more faded snaps of crumbling grounds, players toiling in mud and men in bobble-hats eating pies, you could do worse than have a sneaky bookshop flick through a copy of *What A Shot!* The artistic value of the pics is hilariously mixed, featuring the overexposed back of many a feather cut... but, blown up big, many can take on a strange and wonderful power.

Better still, post your own pics of cavernous Kops, blurred speedy wingers, floodlights and inflatables on the *Got, Not Got* blog. Share a strangely evocative window into a Lost World of Football... from a fans' eye view.

506-8 FILM

3 506-8 FILM

Micky Gynn emerges from garden shed…
hot in pursuit of Big Cyrille Regis.

4 506-8   5 506-8 FILM   3A 06-8 FILM

4 4A 5 5A 6 6A

4 506-8   5 506-8 FILM   6 506-8 FILM

4 4A 5 5A 6

HUMMEL

Although founded in Germany in the 1920s, the sportswear firm Hummel* soon upped and moved to Denmark, and have long been associated with the Danish national side. Their distinctive chevrons were first seen in the UK on football boots and trainers, and then down the sleeves of Crystal Palace, Darlington and Middlesbrough.

At the Mexico 86 World Cup, Hummel unveiled what would become known as the 'Test Card' kit – an eye-boggling, intricate stripy design – for the stylish Denmark side.

All very well for the exotic parade of the World Cup, but it would never catch on over here... or so we thought. For the start of the 1987/88 season, FA Cup winners Coventry, Aston Villa and Southampton all adopted this outrageous design template.

Design Classic or Dog's Dinner? Even after nearly 30 years, the jury's still out!

* Hummel is German for bumblebee, and the logo is a stylised bee, not a funny face. Are we the only people who didn't know this?

The eye-boggling, **intricate stripes** of the 'Test Card' kit.

90 MINUTES

Paul Hawksbee and Dan Goldstein introduced *90 Minutes*, their new independent magazine, as 'The Serious Football Weekly' in April 1990.

Despite this well-timed launch, on the eve of Italia 90, a World Cup that would re-popularise the national sport, for a while it was difficult to see where *90 Minutes* fitted among crowded newsagents' shelves alongside *Shoot!*, *Match* and *When Saturday Comes*.

Paul Hawksbee, now of Talksport radio, explained: "*90 Minutes* started life in March 1990 at 23 Charlton Road, Blackheath, London SE3. Dan Goldstein and I raised five grand through a variety of dubious sources and a further five grand from a friendly NatWest bank. For the first six months it gave us a living and a hefty overdraft so we went looking for help from Dennis Publishing who turned us around, and later IPC whose cash and clout pushed us into the Premier League."

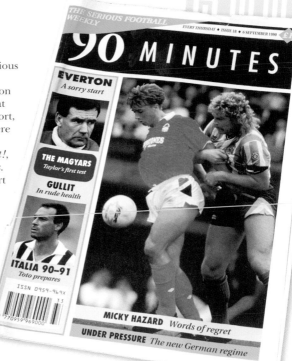

In the IPC years *90 Minutes*, quite literally, became a red-top and developed a humorous approach to the game that was still possible when footballers could still see the joke.

It had a fanzine approach, but with a budget, and proved very popular during the *Loaded*, Brit-Pop, Newman & Baddiel era. Accordingly, the Spice Boys of Anfield – Fowler, Ruddock, Redknapp and McManaman – featured regularly among features like: 'Off the Wall', 'KickBack', 'The Fools' Panel' and 'Very Much So'.

The 359th issue in May 1997 was the last. *90 Minutes* was very much for the Nineties...

Butcher minus characteristic blood: But Tel only played six games in a little over a year as Sky Blues player-boss.

SCOTTISH SUPERSTARS

Up until twenty years ago, every great First Division team in football history had included at least one Scot, usually the brains of the operation – the ball player, the stopper who could do more than just stop, or the unstoppable goalscorer.

The devastating Liverpool side rocked on the fulcrum of Hansen, Souness and/or Dalglish. Dave Mackay was the single most influential player in the Spurs side of the Sixties, then he slotted conclusively into Clough and Taylor's jigsaw at Derby.

Man U had a brilliant boss in Busby, and a European Footballer of the Year in Law – followed by Gordon Strachan, Joe Jordan and Gordon McQueen.

Once upon a time there were Scottish superstars who played all their best football north of the border. Jimmy Johnstone. Jim Baxter. And every generation used to have a stereotypical Scottish leader who invited clichés like Scottish food invites heart disease: 'fearsome warrior' Danny McGrain in his kilt and big, bushy beard; 'Braveheart' Colin Hendry, possibly the last of his kind.

Then there was McLintock, Gray, Nevin, Gemmill, Greig…

To which we're rather proud to be able to add a litany of great servants for the Sky Blues – not a club that many neutrals would instantly associate with Scottish dynasties; but nevertheless one that boasted the aforementioned Strachan in the mid-90s, as the little midfield general made the seamless transition to manager at Highfield Road – and 'Braveheart' as well, toward the end of his career.

Not forgetting Jim Blyth. Willie Carr. Kevin Gallacher. Tommy Hutchison. Eoin Jess. Gary McAllister. David Speedie. Colin Stein. Paul Telfer. Ian Wallace. Gary Gillespie. Jim Holton. Choose fitba.

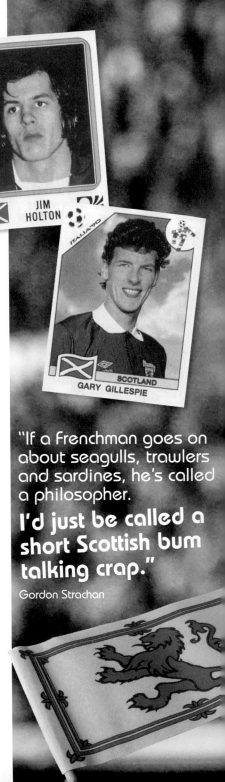

JIM HOLTON

SCOTLAND
GARY GILLESPIE

"If a frenchman goes on about seagulls, trawlers and sardines, he's called a philosopher.

I'd just be called a short Scottish bum talking crap."

Gordon Strachan

SCOTLAND

KEVIN
GALLACHER

TOMMY
HUTCHISON

WM 74

79

Jeff Blockley, City's driving wing-half, and Manchester City winger Mike Summerbee in opposition . . . but the action is in the Cupholders' goalmouth, and visiting 'keeper Joe Corrigan gets to the ball first. Corrigan had a busy time, with City winning 3-0.

FULLY PROGRAMMED Sky Blues v Liverpool - August 26th 1973 - 10p

Joe Mercer Talking

"By the time you are reading this you will know the result of our opening game of the season against the Spurs. But because we had to go to print two days before that game these notes are being penned before I know what happened..."

Sky Blues Opponents

Last season Liverpool won the First Division and the EUFA Cup. Now that's not a bad double by any standards but you can be sure of one thing, manager Bill Shankly will have left his players in no doubt of the fact that last year's deeds have been consigned to the record books.

SKY BLUE

OFFICIAL MAGAZINE OF
COVENTRY CITY F.C. LTD.
OCTOBER 28th
1972
8p

SKY BLUES
v
BIRMINGHAM

Saturday Oct. 28
K.O. 3.00

- - - - - - - -

*Personality
Parade—P13*

Alan Williams
on Birmingham
—Pages 5 and 6

M and B TOP

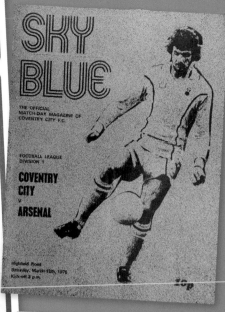

SKY BLUE

THE OFFICIAL
MATCH-DAY MAGAZINE OF
COVENTRY CITY F.C.

FOOTBALL LEAGUE
DIVISION 1

COVENTRY
CITY
v
ARSENAL

Highfield Road
Saturday, March 13th, 1976
Kick-off 3 p.m.

10p

SKY BLUE

OFFICIAL MAGAZINE OF
COVENTRY CITY F.C. LTD.

OCTOBER 20th
1973
10p

21,000

SKY BLUES v WEST HAM | K.O. 3.00

SKY BLUES

IPSWICH

FIRST DIVISION MONDAY 27th DECEMBER 1976
K.O. 3.00 P.M.
OFFICIAL MATCHDAY MAGAZINE
OF COVENTRY CITY F.C.
15p

MBS Bearings

Miller
Bridges
Fastenings

GLENWED

sky blue Magazine

FIRST DIVISION
OFFICIAL MATCHDAY MAGAZINE
OF COVENTRY CITY F.C.
TUESDAY 21ST MARCH, 1978

ASTON VILLA

15p

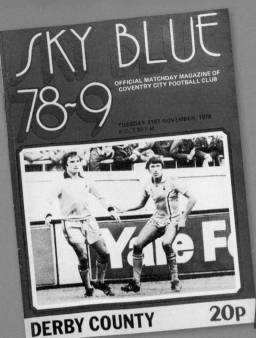

SKY BLUE 78~9

OFFICIAL MATCHDAY MAGAZINE OF
COVENTRY CITY FOOTBALL CLUB

TUESDAY 21ST NOVEMBER, 1978
K.O. 7.30 P.M.

DERBY COUNTY   **20p**

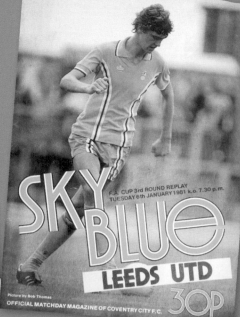

F.A. CUP 3rd ROUND REPLAY
TUESDAY 6th JANUARY 1981 k.o. 7.30 p.m.

SKY BLUE

LEEDS UTD   **30p**

Picture by Bob Thomas

OFFICIAL MATCHDAY MAGAZINE OF COVENTRY CITY F.C.

Meet Your Man
New signing John Craven married his
attractive wife, Christine, four years
ago and they have two children, Mark
and Lee. They hope to be moving to
Finham shortly but have already seen a
lot of the city and like the people.

A lifetime of watching City
As sure as the players keep running out
of the Highfield Road tunnel 84 year old
Charles Harris will be standing on the
Spion Kop supporting his team, as he
has done for 65 years.

"Football is his god. He goes hail,
rain or snow," said Mrs Rose Harris as
she looked up from her knitting.

sky blue

MATCHDAY MAGAZINE

SATURDAY 15th SEPTEMBER 1979 · 3.00 P.M.

Picture by
Bob Thomas

BOLTON   **30p**

OFFICIAL MATCHDAY MAGAZINE OF COVENTRY CITY

SkyBlues

SATURDAY 27th MARCH 1982 k.o. 3.00 p.m.

Picture By Bob Thomas

Official Matchday Magazine
of Coventry City F.C.

v. Wolverhampton Wanderers   **30p**

Sky Blue Shop
Sky Blue Elephant nightdress case - £4.50
Sky Blue Elephant small nightdress case
- £2.30.

Bird's Eye View by Sky Blue Sue
If you feel sluggish when you wake up in
the morning limber up gradually from the
toes upward before you get out of bed.

Player of the Year
Willie Carr, who won the Kleenex-
sponsored Man of the Match first prize
of £250 last season has also been voted
Player of the Year by the City Supporters
Club. He will be presented with a statuette
at an SC function in the near future.

Advert
'Coventry's Front Runners' – Triumph –
Individual cars for individuals.

MATCH WEEKLY

Match Weekly was launched on 6 September 1979, three weeks into the 1979/80 season, by Peterborough-based publishers EMAP. Editor Melvyn Bagnall declared: "Our object is simple... to improve on anything currently available." By which, of course, he meant *Shoot!*, which had enjoyed a relatively unopposed decade of market dominance.

What immediately grabbed this 13-year-old about the newcomer on the newsagent's shelf was the way it was printed right to the edge, making *Shoot!*'s white borders suddenly look very passé.

Inside there was a stellar line-up of writers: Keegan, Clough, Ardiles, Coppell, Atkinson and Jimmy Hill. Instead of 'Focus On' there was 'Match Makers', with loads more questions. There were more colour pages, and 'Match Facts' with marks out of ten for

Cov won the Cup: Dave Bennett and Keith Houchen hoist the trophy Sky Bluewards...

match

KLY · January 31- February 6 1980 · 25p

OPES FOR CHARLIE GEORGE

NEW! **match weekly** · Sept 27-Oct 3 1979 · 25

MAN UNITED SPOTLIGHT
COLOUR POSTERS
DALEY, ARDILES, O'NEILL, GOW
MATCH ACTION
ENGLAND v DENMARK, PALACE v VILLA
Plus CELTIC line-up

Picture Special **KEEGAN** At work and play

A stellar line-up of writers:
Atkinson, Coppell... Jimmy Hill.

every player in every game. And, just
in case anyone was still dithering
about parting with their 25p, there
was a free Transimage sticker
album thrown into the mix.

After a five-year love affair
with *Shoot!*, I jumped ship to
Match in an instant. And I wasn't
the only one. After a long battle,
Match eventually won out with a
higher circulation.

THE DUGOUT

The bench used to be just that. A bench. A modest wooden affair made to seat a maximum of four people. The manager. The trainer, armed with his bucket of cold water and a sponge. The lone substitute, often wearing a sleeping bag in the winter months. Another bloke. Perhaps an injured player wearing a trendy suit. Or an assistant manager wearing a comfortable, battered old tracky top and Rumplestiltskin bottoms.

Subbuteo had it about right with their C114 Bench Set. A beige wooden bench with just three figures on it. No bucket though.

Dugouts were once quite literally pits, dug down to thigh level so as to afford the backroom boys a rubbish view of the match.

Dugouts were once such modest affairs, they were quite literally pits, dug down to thigh level so as to afford the unimportant backroom boys a rubbish view of the match. What mattered most was that paying members of the public could see clearly over their heads.

How times have changed.

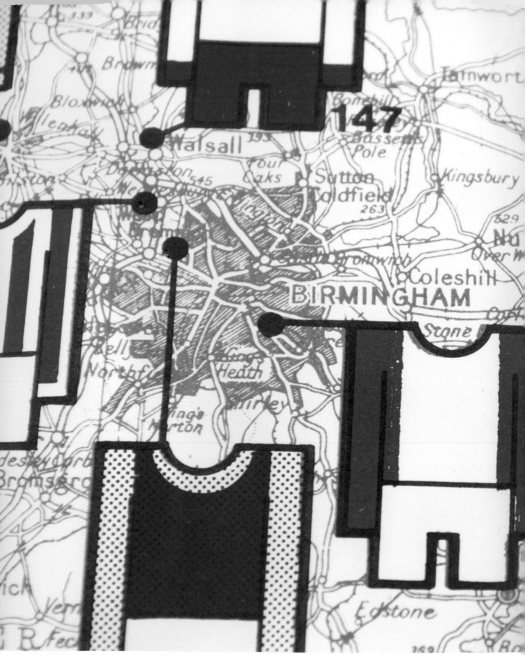

BARTHOLOMEW MAP

In the early 1970s John Bartholomew & Son produced the 'Football History Map of England and Wales' as part of their series of pictorial and historical maps…

Created by John Carvosso, the stylised square kits and re-rendered club crests gave it an iconic look that remains hugely popular among football supporters. In the years just before more intricate kit designs arrived this was all that was required.

It was a best seller among maps which gave a generation of football fans a solid foundation in geography… well,

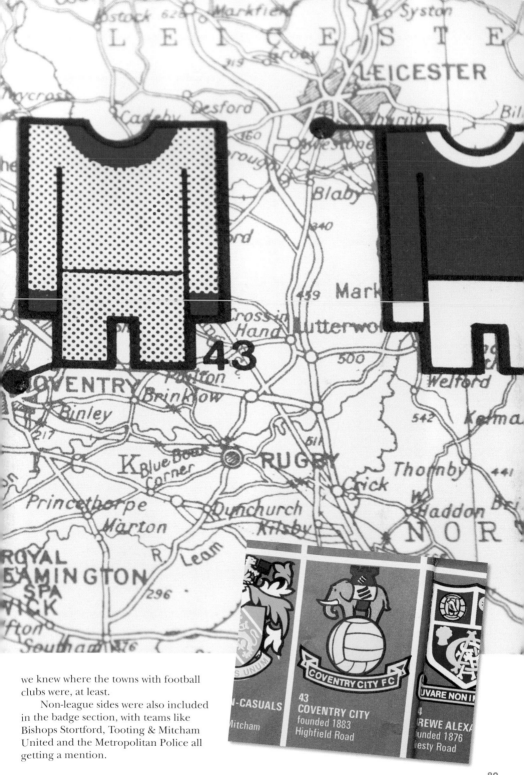

we knew where the towns with football clubs were, at least.

Non-league sides were also included in the badge section, with teams like Bishops Stortford, Tooting & Mitcham United and the Metropolitan Police all getting a mention.

43
COVENTRY CITY
founded 1883
Highfield Road

COVENTRY CITY FC

Back to a time when motoring away used to be a real expedition.

MOTORING AWAY

The sheer naivety of the Coventry City FC furry dice, the Sky Blues mini-kit, the brown-and-chocolate wooden-beaded car seat and the Gordon Milne 'Soundly Grounded' electro-static back-bumper earthing device is enough to whisk you back to a time when motoring away was a real expedition – an adventure and a treat on the A-roads of England when they were cluttered with sky-blue Morris Minors, Hillman Super Minxes and transport caffs galore. Steering sensibly in your string-sided driving gloves, you were magically whisked in the right direction by the *AA Book of the Road*, by stewed cuppas slopped on glass-top tables – and, eventually, the beckoning of floodlight pylons.

It's time to rediscover the joys of a tactical teamtalk with salt and pepper pots in a giant puddle-strewn layby, having followed each and every step of the painstaking directions thoughtfully provided in the previous weekend's home programme.

Saturday, March 10th, 1979
West Bromwich Albion (First Division) Kick-off: 3 p.m.
West Midlands

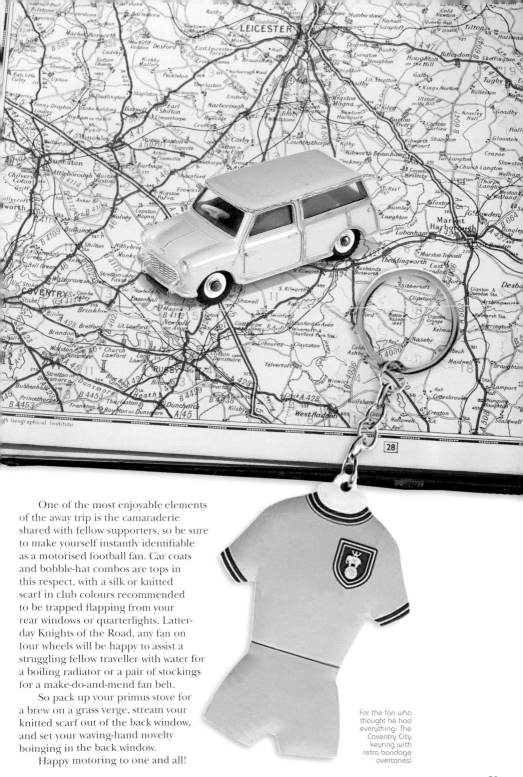

One of the most enjoyable elements of the away trip is the camaraderie shared with fellow supporters, so be sure to make yourself instantly identifiable as a motorised football fan. Car coats and bobble-hat combos are tops in this respect, with a silk or knitted scarf in club colours recommended to be trapped flapping from your rear windows or quarterlights. Latter-day Knights of the Road, any fan on four wheels will be happy to assist a struggling fellow traveller with water for a boiling radiator or a pair of stockings for a make-do-and-mend fan belt.

So pack up your primus stove for a brew on a grass verge, stream your knitted scarf out of the back window, and set your waving-hand novelty boinging in the back window.

Happy motoring to one and all!

For the fan who thought he had everything: The Coventry City keyring with retro bondage overtones!

91

COVBEAT 300

What's the finest City-related choon ever captured on record?

There's not much doubt that 'The Sky Blue Song' is the song best-loved and most closely associated with the club and supporters, but there's never really been a definitive team version banged out on vinyl.

Here's a Top 10 of Sky Blue and Coventry classics.

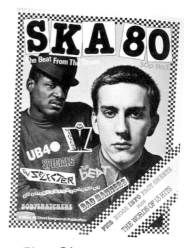

"Let's all sing together, Play up Sky Blues,
While we sing together, They will never lose.
Proud Posh or Cobblers, Oysters or anyone,
They can't defeat them, They'll fight 'til the game is won."

'The Sky Blue Song' – Tune: 'The Eton Boating Song'; Lyrics: Jimmy Hill

1 'GO FOR IT!'
Coventry City FA Cup Final Squad
"Just dug this out of my garage," reported one of our top contributors, lifelong Sky Blue Rich Johnson who runs The Football Attic nostalgia blog. And then he added, somewhat ominously for any record, "Still in perfect condition!"

Ska'd for life: Tommy English and Garry Thompson ham it up, Two-Tone style.

Could this be just the rock 'n' roll cornerstone you're looking for to bring back that 80s feeling? Be wary, however, as Rich warned: "Whatever you do, avoid the B side! You can never unhear it."

2 'GANGSTERS'
The Specials
The focus of cool young Cov's Two-Tone ska obsession in 1979.

3 'JIMMY'S HILL'S SKY BLUES'
Coventry City FC
Bontempi organ 60s singalong from the now-rare Cherry Red Cov football-song compilation CD featuring a handful of genuine club oldies and much modern filler.

4 'THE COVENTRY CITY SONG'
Alan Randall & The Sky Blue Choir
Hot ukulele and football rattle-driven music-hall bash.

5 'STAND UP FOR THE SKY BLUES'
Jim Miekle
Miekle Bolton, more like! Stadium rocktastic anthem.

6 'WHILE THE SKY IS BLUE'
The Believers
1997 single from Cov fans Paul Smith and Mark Boyes, re-released 16 years on to raise spirits.

7 'MOULDY OLD DOUGH'
Lieutenant Pigeon
Number 1 in 1972: local club band featuring Mum tinkling on piano!

GO FOR IT!

The 'SKY BLUES' Song for Wembley FA Cup Final 1987

Photograph courtesy of Coventry Evening Telegraph

8 'ON MY RADIO'
The Selecter

9 'LOVE AND A MOLOTOV COCKTAIL'
The Flies

10 'MY DING-A-LING'
Chuck Berry
Another 1972 number 1, recorded live at Tiffany's Ballroom (now the Library).

BUBBLING UNDER: King, the Primitives and Bolt Thrower!

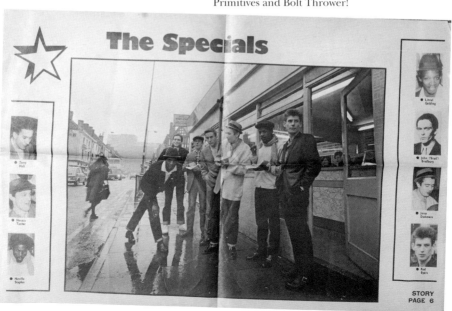

The Specials

STORY PAGE 6

Leeds _____ v _____ Coventry

COLOUR ME BAD

Back in the day, I spent many hours scribbling away at the coarse paper of Caversham's *Football Colouring Book*, tongue lolling out to one side in sheer concentration, transforming the black outlines into lifelike and vibrant living colour. As you can see, I hardly ever went over the lines and had an almost eerie command of every stroke.

Coventry City's sky blue, Liverpool's scarlet, Norwich's brilliant lime-green and yellow, Everton's ultramarine (achieved by pressing a lot harder on the sky blue) were all portrayed to perfection under my artistic spell, now brought to life before your very eyes in a spectral rhapsody.

Just one tiny problem to prick my dreamlike bubble: "WHO'S GOT FELT PEN ON THE CARPET?!"

DOING PENNANTS

Curiously, it's only two classes of games at either end of the importance spectrum – big European matches and Cup Finals, and utterly meaningless friendlies – that attract the attention of the club pennant maker, who provides the skipper with a long triangle of plasticky silk hanging off a length of dowling to hand over to the oppo captain before the toss-up.

Ever was it thus, though exactly why it's impossible to say. It was something to hang in the trophy cupboard during those long barren spells, we suppose. Treasured mementoes of clammy handshakes before the hacking began.

Far more fun than the official jobbies are these cheap plastic pennants designed for children to hang on their walls with less just-pretend po-faced ceremony. It's the ones that you could buy off the market for tuppence which are now worth most to collectors. The ones with the worst-drawn images of silverware and stars, and only partially accurate lists of trophies won before you were born.

Maiden Euro voyage, 70/71: Who saw City beat Trakia Plovdiv and mighty Bayern Munich at home? And who travelled away?

DONATO NARDIELLO

HGT: 5'10"
WGT: 10 st 11 lbs.
BIRTHPLACE: Cardiganshire

WHO AM I?

Captain of Scotland
on their South
American tour

For more...
294 305 3...
Argent...

STRIKER

SEASON 1977-78
CAREER 1972

BARRY POWELL

TOPPS

For anybody who had an American penpal in the 70s, a deep feeling of jealousy always used to accompany the arrival of the aid packages from the Land of the Free, the home of rock 'n' roll, Scooby-Doo, Starsky and Hutch.

We used to send them our unwanted football card and sticker swaps – relatively drab affairs, with baldies kneeling in mud – and by return of post four months later came the most exotic, colourful, glam-rocktastic American football and baseball cards featuring unheard-of megastars with superhero uniforms and names like Ars Blagstrom, Jessie-Bob Jehosephat and Hunk Pfunk.

Then, one day in downtown 1975, poor old A&BC footer cards went bust and were eaten up by US bubble-gum barons Topps.

Almost overnight, our cards grew more exciting, sprouting multi-colours and curlicues originally designed to surround the all-thrusting quarterbacks.

RAY GRAYDON

ALAN GREEN

COVENTRY

JIMMY BLYTH

COVENTRY
DONATO NARDIELLO

MICK FERGUSON
COVENTRY

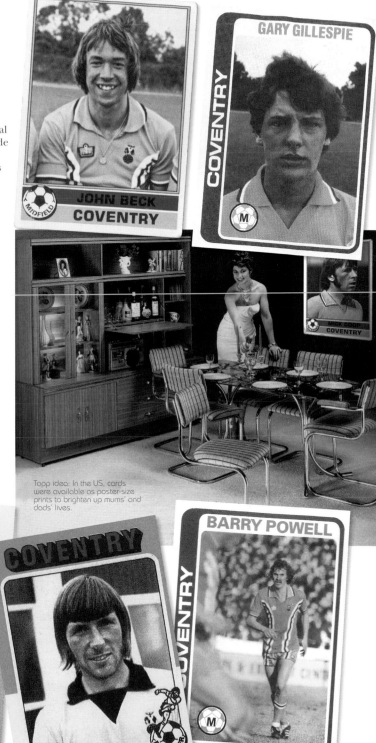

Then the NASL was promoted big in our football comics – a festival of fun with relaxed offside rules and shoot-outs, cheerleaders and players with Captain Kirk beer guts dressed like Evel Knievel. Back-from-the-dead stars played on pitches of lime-green carpet set in towering Space Age kickerdomes.

In America, they played perky organ music when the home team were in possession, and doomy chords when the baddies had the ball. In America they scored six points for a win, not a chiselling two – plus a point per goal scored up to a maximum of three.

But our cool penpals never invited us over.

Topp idea: In the US, cards were available as poster-size prints to brighten up mums' and dads' lives.

...ningham City
...unded 1875.
...93, 1921, 48, 55.
...Cup 1963.
Royal blue

Blackburn Rovers
Founded 1874.
Div 1 1912, 14.
Div 2 1939. FA Cup 1884,
85, 86, 90, 91, 1928.
Blue & white

Blackpool
Founded 1887.
Div 2 1930.
Div 1 runners-up 1956.
FA Cup 1953.
Tangerine & white

Bolton Wanderers
Founded 1874.
Div 2 1909.
FA Cup 1923, 26, 29, 58.
All white

Bradford City
Founded 1903.
Div 2 1908.
Div 3 (N) 1929.
FA Cup 1911.
Claret & amber

Brighton & Hove Albion
Founded 1900.
Div 3 (S) 1958.
Div 1 1965.
Blue & white

Bristol City
Founded 1894.
Div 2 1906.
Div 3 (S) 1923, 27, 55.
All red

Bristol Rovers
Founded 1883.
Div 3 (S) 1953.
Sky blue & white

Everton
...ed 1878. Div 1 1891,
28, 32, 39, 63, 70.
Div 2 1931.
Cup 1906, 33, 66.
Blue & white

Falkirk
Founded 1876.
Sc Div 2 1936, 70.
Sc Cup 1913, 57.
Navy blue & white

Football Club Badges

The Esso collection of 76 famous football club badges.
When you've completed this card you'll have a permanent record of the most famous
football clubs in England, Northern Ireland, Scotland and Wales represented
by their unique and colourful insignias. Keep it safe – you will own what may become
a valuable collector's item.

EC European Cup, ECWC European Cup Winners' Cup, EFC European Fairs Cup, FL Football League, Sc Scottish, SLC Scottish League Cup.

Manchester City
...nded 1894. Div 1 1937.
Div 2 1899, 1903, 10,
47, 66. FA Cup 1904,
56, 69. FL Cup 1970.
...WC 1970. Blue & white

Manchester United
Founded 1878. Div 1 1908,
11, 52, 56, 57, 65, 67.
Div 2 1936. FA Cup 1909,
48, 63. EC 1968.
Red & white

Sunderland
Founded 1879.
Div 1 1892, 93, 95,
1902, 13, 36.
FA Cup 1937.
Red & white

Swansea City
Founded 1911.
Welsh Cup 5 times.
Div 3 (S) 1925, 49.
White & black

Sheffield United
Founded 1889.
Div 1 1898.
Div 2 1953.
...A Cup 1899, 1902, 15, 25.
Red, white & black

Sheffield Wednesday
Founded 1867. Div 1 1903,
04, 29, 30. Div 2 1900,
26, 52, 56, 59.
FA Cup 1896, 1907, 35.
Blue & white

Shrewsbury Town
Founded 1886.
Elected to League 1950.
Welsh Cup twice.
All blue

Southampton
Founded 1885.
Div 3 (S) 1922.
Div 3 1960.
Red, white & black

Stoke City
Founded 1863.
Div 2 1933, 63.
Div 3 (N) 1927.
Red & white

ESSO CLUB BADGES

What was your favourite set of freebies given away with petrol back in the day? Nowadays, it's hard to imagine anything but a form for a mortgage being handed out by the garage man, as it costs the same now to fill your tank as it did to buy your first car. But this hasn't always been the case.

While the likes of Texaco and Shell seemed obsessed with making huge amounts of money by flogging us the world's overflowing natural resources, back in 1971 good old Esso were only concerned with making sure that small boys had plenty of great football stuff to collect. First, there were World Cup coins, then 'Squelchers', a series of little booklets so named because the info contained in them was enough to squelch any argument. There were FA Cup Winners coins, and the Top Team Collection of Photo-Discs built a squad of Britain's best players... but best of all was surely the literally titled 'Esso Collection of Football Club Badges'.

ON THE TOWN

Thanks go out yet again to our number one contributor, Dean Nelson, for this unfakable, irrepressible slice of behind-the-scenes action with three City stars of the 70s. Here's Tommy Hutchison, Ian Wallace and Mick Ferguson out for a polite sherbet at a hostelry where the wallpaper didn't seem to quite match up. Especially if you'd been on the Arctic Lite or the light 'n' lagers since closing time.

"The photo was taken by the landlord's son in the Minstrel Boy pub," Dean explains, "which is in the Allesley area of Coventry and was the 'In' area of Cov at the time.

"It was one o'clock in the morning, as happened regularly back in the day. Tommy Hutchison told me they'd often shut the doors for a lock-in on a Saturday or Monday night.

"Er, did I send you the pic at the same place that has Gary Gillespie with his arm in a sling?"

Esso even provided a splendid fold-out presentation card to stick them in and, frankly, if there was anything more exciting happening in 1971, we can't remember it now. It wasn't just the 20p blackmail job for the 'Starter Pack' of 26 otherwise unobtainable badges that made the heart beat faster. The little foil badges were irresistible. Everyone was collecting them. Have you still got yours?

SKY BLUE GIRL OF THE MATCH

A sincere and heartfelt thanks to all the lovely ladies who featured in this back-of-the-programme glamour spot back in 1972. You all made a huge contribution to the young lives of many a young fan, both home and away, who treasured their Cov programmes of this particular vintage like no other.

Gawd bless you.

BAG TAG

During our time at secondary school we invented a game that was so good we were convinced it would be adopted by every twelve-year-old boy in the land, sweeping across Britain like a forest fire; but somehow it didn't.

All you need is an Adidas bag
(with 'all day I dream about sex' added in felt pen).

All you needed to make dinner-hour a time of high-octane excitement was a tennis ball. The rest of the equipment you already lugged round with you all day. Your bag.

Whether the cheapo variety with 'Sports' printed on the side; or a pricier 'Adidas' bag (with 'all day I dream about sex' added in felt pen) we placed them in a circle, the size of which was determined by the number of players. The rules were simple, as indeed were we. You could only touch the ball with your feet. Your bag was your own individual goal. If the ball hit your bag you had one life left – a second hit and you were out of the game. You had to strike a balance between defending your own bag and forming alliances to attack someone else's. There was plenty of scope for subterfuge and double bluff and just as in *Macbeth* (which we would be studying later that day in English), overreaching ambition could swiftly lead to your downfall.

Trevor Peake up against
Leeds at Hillsborough
**on the road to
Wembley, 1987.**

"Regis... Houchen...
Bennett... Houchen!

Brilliant goal!
Keith Houchen

WEMBLEY STADIUM

TURNSTILES
H
ENTRANCE
62

801 WEST
LOWER
Football Association
Challenge Cup Final Tie
SAT., 16 MAY, 1987
KICK-OFF 3.00 p.m.
YOU ARE ADVISED TO TAKE UP
YOUR POSITION BY 2.30 p.m.

1. This ticket is not transferable. 2. This counter-
foil must be retained for at least 6 months.

STANDING
ENCLOSURE

STANDING   £6.00

TO BE RETAINED

ISSUED SUBJECT TO THE
CONDITIONS ON BACK

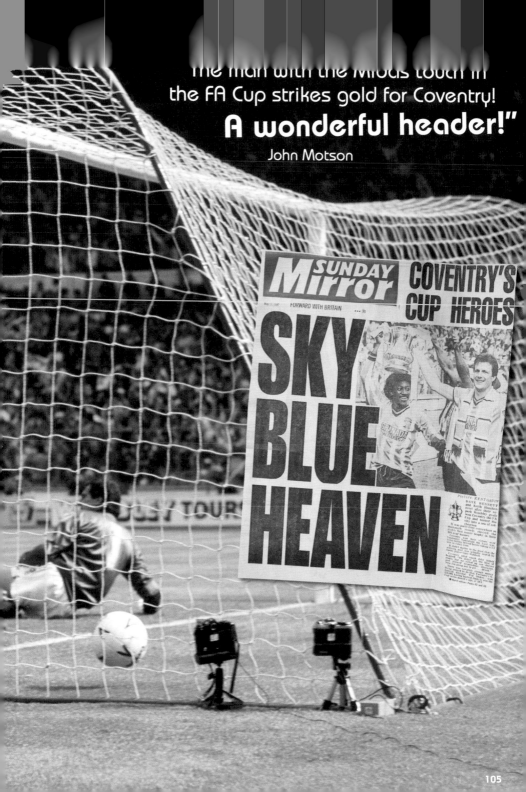

"The man with the Midas touch in the FA Cup strikes gold for Coventry!

A wonderful header!"

John Motson

WEMBLEY

"Based on the English Football Association Challenge Cup Competition, the most gripping features and exciting uncertainties of which it reproduces with vivid and truly amazing fidelity..."

No one plays board games any more: it's all down to attention span and lack of imagination and wanting excitement served up on a plate instead of having to work at it. And that's just us, never mind the kids.

"Good luck ! May the dice roll well for you, and may your favourite team appear many times in the final of the Cup at WEMBLEY."

It was the thrill of the Cup draw and the possibility of an alternate-universe upset that used to make Wembley so addictive. The reproduction of all those associations and assumptions that electrify the simple twinning of two clubs' names ("And it's Coventry... at home to... Leeds United"... or "Accrington Stanley"... or "Everton"... we could go on).

It was the tension inherent in the inevitable reduction of 32 clubs to an historic final pairing. The chance to witness a spunky lower-league outfit confound the Darwinian bias that enabled top clubs to make more money, to spend it on star players, to score more goals... and even claim the right

to throw loaded dice.

"The earning ability of clubs varies greatly, as does their playing ability," stated the Rules of the Game. "Each club has a value (representing gate receipts) and each Division has different colour dice for Home and Away matches. These dice are specially produced to give a built-in advantage both to teams in higher divisions and to teams playing at Home."

The powerful red First Division Home die could roll 0, 1, 2, 3 or two chances of a 4, while the white Third/Fourth Division Away die was lumbered with two 0s and two 1s – plus a potentially giant-killing 4 and a 5 to spice things up.

MONTY GUM CARDS

Nestling, unloved, in a corner of my football card box was a wodge of these 'Football' cards from 1975/76 – an undistinguished set with an indistinctive title, featuring a picture of a football and another picture of a football.

Turn them over for details and you were met with a blank greyness of card of a similar quality to that of a cereal box.

They really weren't giving much away, with no numbers and only the players' surnames. Many of these were spelt wrong - City got off relatively lightly with 'Hundley' and 'Greene'.

I disliked them for their laissez-faire attitude towards details and information, but not enough to throw them away.

Only with the advent of the internet did we learn that they were produced by a company called 'Monty Gum' based in Holland.

I actually quite like them now.

City got off relatively lightly with 'Hundley' and 'Greene'.

PROSET

Some time after the Golden Age of football cards, a new collection made by 'Proset' was suddenly launched during the 1990/91 season. They were a good looking set, covering City's 'Asics' period and a second series was brought out the following season.

Though the first set was branded with the FA badge, the second one carried the Football League logo, though that institution was on the verge of losing its biggest clubs to the newly formed Premier League and a third collection did not appear.

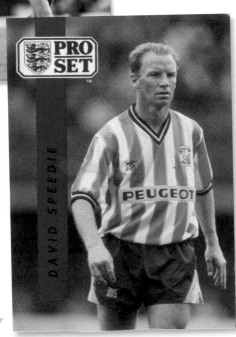

Speedo: Nearly four years at Cov saw the pugnacious striker drop effectively into a deeper midfield role.

Only with the advent of the internet did we discover that 'Proset' was a US company belonging to Lud Denny, a former pilot and oil operator who took a punt on producing sports cards and ending up doing $165 million of business in a year.

Denny said of his 44,000-square-foot headquarters: "We're getting to be a reasonably sized lemonade stand."

After producing cards for American Football, hockey and golf he turned his attention to "Soccer".

It appears he had learned a lesson from the generation before him as they turned their sights on Hitler: "Basically, England is a stepping stone into the rest of Europe..."

THE COACH AND THE BOSS

We asked Gordon Milne about the old debate regarding managers and coaches, and whether you can be both. A half-decent question, given that he started out as coach under Joe Mercer, then graduated to manager himself…

"There are people who are definitely coaches," Gordon replied. "People like Ron Wylie who was with me at Coventry. Their day and their week is planned around what we're going to do out there on the training ground. That in itself is a job. Managers can flit in and out of that, but they've got other problems and responsibilities. A lot of people find that they are fine with the coaching but the other aspects of management prove too much for them. It is a big workload and it takes them away from what they enjoy doing, which is being out there with the players."

GNG: Are you talking about yourself here?!

GM: I was quite lucky when I went to Coventry. I moved there from non-league Wigan (who are now in the big time, of course) with Joe Mercer. The big appointment was Joe Mercer who had the reputation, while nobody knew who I was, coming from the non-league. But I was the coach and I was the one who picked the team. Joe was a buffer between me and the board and the media. It was invaluable to me in the early stages.

GNG: Being a manager must be the loneliest job.

GM: You can find that you don't have too many people to talk to. You need someone to back you up but you have to be careful who you choose. You don't want someone who is after your job, or someone who is in the chairman's pocket. It's not easy is it?

There has always been an awful lot of pressure on managers, but it is even worse these days!

IN THE PINK

This same ritual went on up and down the country for decades, little kids and old blokes queuing up outside the paper shop at 6 o'clock on Saturday night, waiting for the sports final edition of the local paper – the *Green 'Un*, the *Pink 'Uns*, the *Blue 'Un* or the *Buff*. Any colour as long as it wasn't white. Here was sports journalism at its most demanding, where reports were phoned in on the hoof, assumptions were made before the final whistle, and last-minute goals were any editor's nightmare.

The *Evening Telegraph Sports Final* was vital reading for those fans who couldn't rest until they had read

The Pink match report
was vital reading
if you'd just left Highfield Road 80 minutes ago.

a report of a game that some of them had seen eighty minutes ago (unless they were after confirmation of a result they'd just heard played out on the radio).

The *Pink* gave you the chance to settle down in a favourite armchair, to check the pools and peruse the results and league tables at your leisure. In the days before Sky News and even Ceefax, it was either this or wait for the arrival of the Sunday papers.

Gradually the need for a Saturday evening sports edition lessened and then disappeared altogether. The internet was one blow – suddenly you didn't need to be standing out on the street in January – but the killer was the spreading of fixtures over the weekend due to the demands of TV.

One by one, the sports papers had to admit defeat and hold up their hands in surrender, in Manchester and Liverpool, Leicester and Birmingham... although the Norwich *Pink 'Un* and Ipswich's *Green 'Un* are both websites now.

If you can't beat 'em, join 'em.

THE FOOTBALL CARD ENGINE

Here's how to transform your humble pushbike into a revved-up, throbbing beast of a motorcycle, all too easy to mistake for a 750cc Norton Commando (provided you're only listening rather than looking).

All you need is:

1 – One giant pile of football cards;
2 – Two clothes pegs;
3 – An anti-social desire to terrorise your neighbours like those cool Hells Angels you've seen on *Nationwide*; and,
4 – A tragic disregard for your future financial security.

If you've got a teetering pile of cards, it naturally follows that you've got an even bigger pile of swaps, collected up over weeks of frustration while searching for the two or three you need for the set.

Transform your pushbike into a Hells Angel's Norton Commando

with David Cross's woody thrum.

We recommend you use a David Cross 'blue-back' from Topps's 1976/77 'Footballer' series. He's got a nice woody thrum.

All you have to do is use the pegs to secure the cards on to your bike frame so they stick a little way into the spokes. Then push off, taking note of the unusual sensation of slight resistance as you wobble down the gutter, turning heads with a guttural, engine-like *Vrrrrrrrrp*.

This way, in one afternoon you might easily burn through £100's worth of future sought-after collectables at 21st-century prices. But what the heck. You're only young once, eh?

Did you know? 70s netminder Bryan King now lives in Norway and is a scout for Everton…

CLUB SHOP

Be sure and visit the Coventry City FC Megastore the next time you drop by the Ricoh. That way, you can walk out of the deal with an attractive calendar of the playing staff as of last July (which was out of date by the start of the season), a corporate badged grooming set (eyebrow notcher; beard sculptor; hair, shower and lubricant gel) or a bargain black nylon T-shirt worth 3 quid (today, all third kits are either black or grey. Why? Because they 'look good with jeans' according to the PR man.

But hey, all sizes other than XXL and XXXL are reduced to a mere 30 quid! Which is to say, 50 quid to you.)

There's a lot more going on at every Football League ground than kicking a ball around these days. We're talking delights such as business-class banqueting, stadium tours, a hotel with rooms overlooking the pitch, a members-only gym, conference facilities and unlimited retail opportunities.

Bring back the old souvenir shop, where they only sold plastic caps, sew-on patches and programme binders. None of your new-fangled showy stuff like mugs, mind. And no need for bobble hats, because that's what grans were for.

What price the return of the half-price back-issue programme box?

Items	Price	Postage
Coventry City rings	35	5
Coventry City cuff links	£1.15	4
Coventry City pendants	85	8
Coventry City bracelets	85	8
Coventry City ash trays	45	4
Coventry City pennants	25	4
Other 1st Div clubs pennants	25	4
Other 1st Div clubs enamel badges	25	4
College type scarf	£1.50	5
Coventry City satin scarf	70	5
Coventry City green and black	90	5
Coventry City airline bag	£1.40	20
Sky Blue elephant nightdress case	£4.50	26
Sky Blue elephant small nightdress case	£2.30	20
Coventry City ties	£1.25	4
Coventry City rosettes	15	5

Above are some of the items on sale in our Sky Blue Shops. For a full list of souvenirs available please write enclosing a S.A.E. to: Sky Blue Shop, Main Stand, King Richard St., Coventry. The figure given under postage includes packing, and the extra cost must be included with any order. Fill in the order form and tick articles required.

ORDER NOW!

◁ Stick on car teddy	£
Spikey the hedgehog car fresheners	£
Home & away flat cap	£
White printed mug	£
Yellow and black Jacquard scarf	£
Tankards	pint £
	half £2.25 mini
Printed scarf	£
Slippers	childs £
	youths £6.50 adults £
Romper suits	£
Gloves	childs £
	youths/adults £

PLAQUE ATTACK

Collect the Big Names Now!

And, with all due respect to Darlington and Southport, some of the smaller ones, too.

Once you'd cut out your first token from this *Shoot!* advert, ripped another off a fish-finger box and painstakingly assembled 25 new pee, then you were ready to send off and claim your embossed football club plaque from the Co-Op.

City were safely on the seemingly random list of 31 large, medium and frankly tiddler-sized clubs.

It's All at Your Co-Op... NOW!

However, somewhat oddly, these vital tribal territory markers were also presented as a Typhoo Tea promotion a year later, in the 1972/73 season, with a similar wedge of two tokens and 25p required.

Collect the big names now!

EMBOSSED CLUB PLAQUES

Only 25p and 2 tokens from special Co-op packs

And getting the tokens is as easy as doing the shopping because they're on all kinds of Co-op products from cream crackers to fish fingers. To help you get started here's your first Football Plaque Token free! Full details of where to post etc., are on all the special Co-op Football Token packs. Watch out for them. The large plaque shown here is actual size, and the full list of plaques available is:

Leeds	Wolves	Notts. Forest	Oldham
Manchester United	Birmingham	Hull	Peterborough
Arsenal	West Brom.	Portsmouth	Shrewsbury
Chelsea	Millwall	Coventry	Darlington
Liverpool	Sheffield United	Charlton	Southport
West Ham	Newcastle	Bristol City	Stockport
Manchester City	Sheffield Wednesday	Luton	Middlesbrough
	Southampton	Lincoln	

(If your club is not listed, write to the address on Co-op label packs for further information)

YOUR FIRST ONE FREE!
(Only 1 free token accepted per plaque)

at **your** Co-op now!

CO OP

A second chance to stick one firmly to the outside of your bedroom door with four foam Sellotape sticky fixers. That baby was never coming off in one piece...

113

Let's have a look at the old scoreboard... The first in the Football League!

COVENTRY EV

Hird·Brown SKY BLU
LEEDS UT

THE SCOREBOARD

Not long ago, while at a match, I was checking on the scores of the oppo on Livescore.com. It was taking a little longer to download than usual (probably about eight-tenths of a second) and I was poking the screen of my iPhone in an exasperated fashion.

A few short years back, before we carried around the collective knowledge of the world in the palm of our hand, we had to wait until half-time to see how the other games were going. Then they'd be viewed on the electronic scoreboard, accompanied by boos or

late Sixties (which now appears technologically equidistant between the Saxons and Samsung) most grounds employed a simple but effective code which allowed supporters to see the scores around other grounds. It involved a chap with a wooden box full of metal plates with numbers on them, arranging them next to a row of letters, usually situated on the front wall of a stand. In the days when a programme cost a shilling, everybody bought one, and you turned to the appropriate page to crack the code.

And, somehow, we got by.

ADMIRAL

The Admiral brand could be traced back to 1914 when it was used by the Leicester underwear concern, ABC Hosiery Ltd. By the 1970s the company were called Cook & Hurst Ltd., based in the suburb of Wigston.

At this time the first manufacturers' logos were beginning to appear on football shirts, and it was Admiral who seized on the possibilities of

commercialising strips. Bert Patrick, chairman of Cook & Hurst, had formed an idea born out of England's 1966 World Cup win and the advent of colour TV. If kits could be uniquely designed and visibly branded then contracts with clubs could be signed, and the parents of young football fans would have to buy Admiral kit rather than the plain, generic shirts currently available. With a young, go-getting sales force, Admiral set about conquering the domestic market.

Don Revie's fondness for making a bit of brass to supplement his salary at Leeds was a big help in the early days. Leeds were the first to wear the nautical trademark. Then, when Revie became England boss, a £16,000 deal was cut and England's traditional plain white shirt was suddenly adorned with red-and-blue sleeve stripes and a yellow logo, much to the horror of traditionalists and to the delight of schoolboys across the nation. That shirt was the must-have item of 1975, and when Manchester United were also signed up, Admiral had the 'Big Three'. The rest quickly fell into line.

That's when Coventry City were signed up. In 1975/76, the players got to sport Admiral logos, and plenty of them. Dads recoiled with horror when they saw Admiral's typically unrestrained 'tramline' design. It was the end of football as we knew it, they reckoned. And they were probably right. But kids loved the jazzy nautical logos on their shirts and shorts – closely followed by their socks!

The Admiral agents had an eye for an opportunity. When Southampton beat Manchester

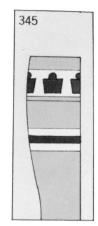

345

United in the 1976 FA Cup Final they wore an Admiral strip that had been designed and manufactured since their semi-final victory, and the multiple logos down sleeves and shorts were exposed to a huge global TV audience.

In every copy of *Shoot!* there would be a full-page colour advert showing their latest designs; there was an *Admiral Annual* which showed only photos of games in which both sides wore the approved brand; and you could send away for a giant poster which displayed the company's growing roster of clubs from Aberdeen and Dundee to Orient and Eintracht Frankfurt.

Sky Blues boss Gordon Milne meets his bespoke outfitter and style consultant, Admiral boss Bert Patrick.

In commercial terms, Admiral had done such a great job by 1977, they were hauled over the coals in Parliament by Newport MP Roy Hughes:

"My object is to focus attention on the undesirable practices of certain sports equipment manufacturers," he complained. "The most unpleasant aspect is that children are being exploited. Star-struck youngsters who wish to wear the colours of their favourite teams are having to pay through the nose for the pleasure."

The general opinion of the Commons was that it was all a jolly rotten do, but there was nothing they could do about it. But Admiral, having lived by the sword of commerce, would soon die by it.

Inevitably, Adidas, Umbro and Le Coq Sportif caught up with, and overtook, the pioneering Admiral. By the early Eighties, they'd lost their roster of bigger clubs, and the England contract, the biggest in world football, had moved to Umbro. Its brief Golden Age over, the company sadly went bust.

"Star-struck youngsters wearing the colours of their favourite teams are having to pay through the nose for the pleasure."

Something
on your mind!
Drop a line to GOAL
Lines. Praising or pan-
ning, it doesn't matter.
£3 for Star Letter.
Address: GOAL Lines,
GOAL, 161/166 Fleet
St., London,
E.C.4.

GOAL

Modestly subtitled 'The World's Greatest Soccer Weekly', *Goal* launched on 16 August 1968, with a right posh do at the Savoy with dolly birds and everything.

Its distinctive covers, with a bright yellow title on a red background and circular photo design, owed a nod to pop art, and they've stood the test of time, still looking fresh and bold to this day.

'Opinion' kicked things off – "There is no sitting on the fence with Tommy Docherty. You are either for him or very much against him" – though 'Bobby Charlton's Diary' was the undoubted star turn. And then editor Alan Hughes reflected on the important matters of the day: "Birmingham City are an odd team."

Amid more distinctively designed colour posters, 'Booter', the Beatle-haired footballer starred in his own cartoon strip; and we got to 'Meet the Girl behind the Man'.

Goal became a victim of its own success because exactly a year later, encouraged by decent sales, IPC introduced a second football weekly, entitled *Shoot!*

Although both went on to achieve healthy circulations of around 220,000 by 1971, *Goal* then went into decline, and its 296th and final issue came out two weeks before the start of the 1974 World Cup.

It was then 'incorporated' into *Shoot!* which was akin to having to sleep under your little brother's bed. Oh, the indignity.

BOBBY CHARLTON on LEEDS and C

Dave Clements: £1,500 bargain from Wolves, 48 caps for Northern Ireland…

THE TACKLE FROM BEHIND

There would appear to be some
confusion regarding the tackle from
behind, and whether or not it has
been outlawed. In 2005, FIFA removed
the phrase "from behind" from the
laws of the game, replacing it with "a
tackle which endangers the safety of an
opponent," which was to be "sanctioned
as serious foul play."

With this change, it seemed
that uncompromising defenders
and combative midfielders would
immediately have 180 degrees restored
to their field of operations, but sadly that
isn't way things panned out. T-boneadly
that isn't way things panned out.

Because the tackle from behind is a
challenge you don't see coming – that

would only spoil the surprise – there's no chance, no time to get your feet off the ground, which means an increased chance of injury. And this applies even if the defender does manage to get a toe-end to the ball a millisecond before he sends you twelve feet in the air.

TOP TEAMS

In 1971, the good people at Marshall Cavendish, of Old Compton Street, launched their *Book of Football* a part-work encyclopaedia in 75 issues.

To ensure that you kept buying these weekly parts at a cool 23p (*Shoot!* was only 6p at this time) an extra incentive was nailed on to the deal.

In part two you got this *Book of Football – Top Teams* album and each week a sheet of 16 'stickers' in random order was issued. After carefully cutting them out with the big scissors from your Mam's sewing basket they were ready to be glued in.

They had you trapped now, for your quid a month.

Only when all your City heroes were present and correct on their page could you relax once more.

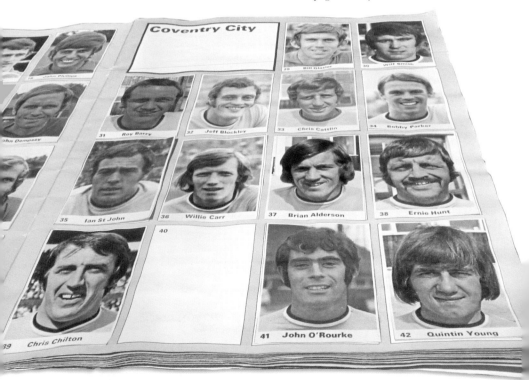

THE VIDEO AGE

Seldom has a new technology flared so brightly and died so quickly as video.

The race to develop a consumer-level video system was run in 1970s Japan, with JVC and their VHS eventually managing to overshadow Sony's Betamax system, and by 1978 the first video players were available in the UK. Available, but far from affordable for all but the spoilt kids.

Most families got one some time in the middle of the Eighties. It's pretty easy to work out because that's when our magpie collections of *Match of the Day* on Kodak E-180 tapes begins – not forgetting *Saint & Greavsie* and *Football Focus* editions snagged for posterity, when the ability to capture moving pictures off the telly box still seemed like something out of *Buck Rogers in the 25th Century*.

Whether painstakingly taping goals from the regional news, or building up a video library that could be measured in yards, it was an obsessive, and ultimately a pitifully pointless exercise.

No one now plays their rare early white-label editions of black-and-white match footage from City's successes in the late Sixties, never mind *Danny Baker's Own Goals and Gaffs* and the endless run of season highlights from seasons that somehow now seem to all run together in the mind. They're all out in the garage now, along with the precious unplayed

vinyl and the music cassettes and the slideshow projector and the magic vegetable peeler gimmicks, still mint and boxed up the same as the day you bought them.

One day, the plan is to get a special machine where you link it up to your computer and convert them all into DVDs. One day...

Video tech: imagine a DVD printed out on a long strand of tinsel, spooled up in a plaggy case.

sky blue

MATCHDAY MAGAZINE
SATURDAY 15TH DECEMBER 1979 – 3.00 p.m.

MANCHESTER UTD 30p
OFFICIAL MATCHDAY MAGAZINE OF COVENTRY CITY F.C.

From us to you:
Have a very happy
Christmas, and a
splendid New Year
in 1979.

Subbuteo.
Team

XMAS MORNING

Our 1970s Christmases, in our terrace
front rooms and boxy housing-estate
semis, weren't quite the same as the
sumptuous Victorian festivals portrayed
on Christmas cards and chocolate
boxes, in TV ads and cartoons.
　　We didn't have stockings hanging
from huge holly-bedecked fireplaces.
　　　We had striped pillowcases stuck on
the end of our beds.
　　　　We didn't have
gaily laughing guests –
　　　gentlemen in top hats

SEASONS
GREETINGS

124

and ladies wearing furry muffs – we had bald men round in their new V-neck jumpers, and they hardly spoke.

And we had, to be frank, shite artificial Christmas trees, not those towering, richly decorated spruces portrayed on the cover of the *Radio Times*.

As for the romantic notion of a White Christmas, it never snowed round our way; though sometimes it rained.

Christmas dinner was the same as normal Sunday dinner, except with turkey instead of roast beef, and with added parsnips and sprouts. Rather than the mouthwatering spreads portrayed ... well, you get the idea.

But somehow, on Christmas morning, with Noel Edmonds visiting

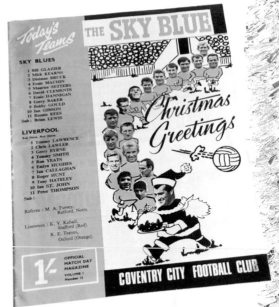

We never had sleds and holly-bedecked fireplaces
but, then, they never had Subbuteo Team No. 172, did they?

children in hospital as a televisual backdrop, we still managed to reach a goosebump-inducing level of excitement.

And it was all because we knew that, concealed in cheap Woolies wrapping paper, piled up under the shite tree, there lurked *Shoot!* annuals, Wembley Trophy footballs, full football strips and Subbuteo accessories housed in their pale green boxes.

So we never took a horse-drawn sled down to the pine forest to chop down the tallest tree to place by the main staircase like those privileged Victorians... but then, they never had Subbuteo Team No. 172, did they?

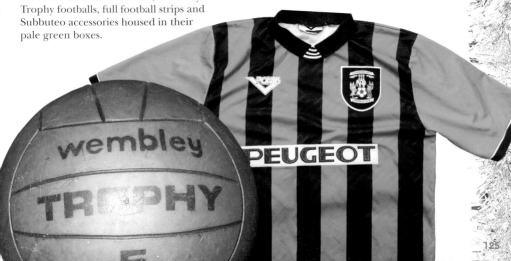

Authors

Gary Silke and Derek Hammond are the authors of *The Lost World of Football* (Pitch, 2013); *What A Shot! Your Snaps of the Lost World of Football* (Pitch, 2013), and *Got, Not Got: The A-Z of Lost Football Culture, Treasures & Pleasures* (Pitch, 2011).

Picture Credits

Acknowledgments

Thanks to Dean Nelson, Sky Blues supercollector, for a huge amount of personal memorabilia – badges, mugs, progs, scarves, scrapbooks, tickets, videos, pennants, personal photos, records and more – without whom this book would not have been possible.

Richard Johnson for the second large pile of fantastic Sky Blue clutter which we've arrayed lovingly on these pages. We're talking Subbuteo, snaps at the match, shirts, programmes and loads more. Check out Rich's excellent retro football blog at thefootballattic.blogspot.com.

Steve Phelps, author of the recommended *Coventry City Miscellany* and a forthcoming book about the great 1987 adventure. Look out for *Play up Sky Blues: The Year Coventry Sang Together* in 2015!

Neville Evans, owner of the National Football Shirt Collection, for the Tallon shirt – and Simon 'Shakey' Shakeshaft for all his help.

Duncan Olner, our ever-patient designer, lifelong Sky Blue and provider of many tasty photographic sundries.

Paul Woozley, the proprietor of the excellent oldfootballgames.co.uk website, who let us take photos of, and even play with, all his great stuff.

Nigel Mercer for his Lion league ladders and his Sky Blues Co-Op plaque. Check out his ace, encyclopaedic football card and sticker website at cards.littleoak.com.au.

Gordon Milne for our interview.

The Coventry City Football Book

DEREK HENDERSON
Foreword by Noel Cantwell

Critical Acclaim for *The Lost World of Football*

"Wonder at the unreconstructed non-PC days when Manchester City bikinis were on sale in the Maine Road club shop, when a top-selling football annual promoted Park Drive cigarettes, and when Coventry City invited their more photogenic female fans to be 'our girl of the match' in the programme. Just as *Got, Not Got* invited the reader on an irresistible meander down Memory Lane, *The Lost World Of Football* is no easier to put down."
Backpass

"The authors have put so much into this book - it's a mixture of remarkable photographs, toys, stickers, club icons, and not forgetting the writing - it's beautiful!"
Andy Jacobs, talkSPORT

"A hugely evocative pictorial memorial to the innocence of a game before it became a business. Each page filled with the iconic paraphernalia of a homespun fandom that shaped a generation's adolescence but allowed us the space to make our own dreams."
The Morning Star

"This book is superb."
Steve Anglesey, The Mirror

"Should you yearn for the days of petrol station freebies and naff endorsements (Trevor Brooking patio doors, anyone?), you'll love this celebration of clutter and culture. Packed with evocative pictures, younger readers can rejoice in the fact that they've never received Kevin Keegan slippers in their stocking. Great fun."
FourFourTwo

"Brilliant!"
Sport magazine

"There's a whole series of books called Got, Not Got: brilliant books looking back at old football memorabilia."
James Brown, talkSPORT

"The original *Got, Not Got* was a masterpiece, so the pressure was really on to come up with the goods yet again. Would there possibly be enough to fill another book? The answer is of course, yes. Not just a small yes, but a rather large one – and also a bunch of club-specific volumes and a further gem in the guise of *What a Shot: Your Snaps of the Lost World of Football*. A truly beautiful thing, a phrase which neatly sums up the *Lost World of Football*."
Fly Me To The Moon fanzine

"The book is superb – an actual step up, if possible, on *Got, Not Got*. Got it, love it... lost about five hours at the weekend!"
In Bed With Maradona

"It's the football book equivalent of *The Godfather II* or *Toy Story 2* – the same, but arguably even better than the original *Got, Not Got*. On every page, there was something to remember or something I'd never heard of but wish I'd owned back in the day. On every page a gasp or a titter. Lavishly illustrated, brilliantly written, *The Lost World of Football* is a thoroughly engrossing read from cover to shining cover."
Hopping Around Hampshire blog

"*The Lost World of Football* is a must-have for fans, a sought-after stocking filler."
Mirror.co.uk